"Nowhere is the daze that swings between exultation and extinction in early motherhood better described. Amanda Lamb's raw, tender, bone-honest truths drive home that some things would be too difficult—if we didn't do them out of love."

—Jacquelyn Mitchard, author of *Still Summer*
and *The Deep End of the Ocean*

"Amanda Lamb stands out as the new voice for momhood—not scared to say that parenting is not only sometimes scary but often laugh-out-loud hilarious, even raucous, but always tender, and always riding the whitewaters of love."

—Hollis Gillespie, author of
*Bleachy-Haired Honky Bitch*

"A must-read for working moms. Amanda Lamb beautifully captures the chaos that is her life as a mother and a TV journalist."

—Mika Brzezinski, MSNBC anchor/
NBC News contributor

"Amanda Lamb is a hard-charging, pull-no-punches veteran television reporter. *Smotherhood* doesn't pull any punches either. It is her story of the wrestling match with the demands of motherhood, marriage, and a very busy career, told in a way that is unabashed, honest, and frank."

—Mary P. Easley, JD, First Lady of North Carolina

"For manic, multi-tasking mothers everywhere! Amanda's tales will make you laugh—and remind you to enjoy this crazy journey."

—Jane Skinner, anchor, Fox News Channel

*Wickedly Funny Confessions from the Early Years*

AMANDA LAMB

GUILFORD, CONNECTICUT
AN IMPRINT OF THE GLOBE PEQUOT PRESS

To buy books in quantity for corporate use
or incentives, call **(800) 962–0973**,
or e-mail **premiums@GlobePequot.com**.

· · · · · · · · · · · · · · · · · · · · · · · · · · · · · · · · · · · · · · · · · · · ·

skirt! books are all about women—spirited, unpredictable, independent, sometimes controversial, always passionate.

*Smotherhood* is a trademark of the author, used by permission.

skirt!® is an imprint of The Globe Pequot Press.
skirt!®, a registered imprint of Morris Communications, LLC, is used with express permission.

10  9  8  7  6  5  4  3  2  1

Printed in the United States of America

Designed by Jane Sheppard

Page layout by Sheryl P. Kober

**Library of Congress Cataloging-in-Publication Data**
Lamb, Amanda.
    Smotherhood : wickedly funny confessions from the early years / Amanda Lamb.
        p. cm.
    ISBN-13: 978-1-59921-208-1
    ISBN-10: 1-59921-208-0
    1. Motherhood. 2. Motherhood—Anecdotes. 3. Mothers—Psychology. 4. Mother and child. I. Title.
    HQ759.L34 2007
    306.874'3—dc22
                                                      2007004872
· · · · · · · · · · · · · · · · · · · · · · · · · · · · · · · · · · · · · · · · · · · ·

*To My Family—Grif, Mallory, and Chloe*

# ontents

# Acknowledgments

I would like to thank my husband, Grif, and my daughters, Mallory and Chloe, for allowing me the time and space to follow my dreams even when the work required me to take precious time and energy away from them. I lovingly thank them for allowing me to share our imperfect, wonderful life with the rest of the world in the hopes that others may relate to our flaws and get a good laugh in the process.

I especially thank my parents, who taught me that I could be anything I wanted to be when I grew up; it just took awhile! I also thank them for allowing me to tenderheartedly poke fun at their imperfections—imperfections that make them human and even more lovable to me.

I thank my agent Sharlene Martin for her passion, tenacity and professionalism in helping me to realize my dream.

To Globe Pequot Press and all of the people at skirt! who gave me a chance to make it happen and worked hard to make me look good in the process—editors Mary Norris and Amy Paradysz, and the very creative designers Jane Sheppard and Sheryl P. Kober.

And to my friend John, who told me to "be a writer" instead of just talking about it. Thanks for the advice—I took it!

# Prologue

*"Most of us become parents long before
we have stopped being children."*
—Mignon McLaughlin

"Why can't I ride my bike in the street by myself?"

Her entire body pleaded with me. Even the mismatched shirt stained with red juice, the oversize T-shirt skirt, and the purple plastic leopard-printed flip-flops seemed to be chiding me, begging me to give in.

"Because it's not safe," I said, rewrapping the wet baby in my arms in her bath towel. My head pounded from too little sleep.

"*My* mom lets me do it," snorted Mallory's little friend, who had wedged herself halfway inside the front door of our house to join the debate. "It's really okay," she said, smugly cocking her head to keep her loosely fitting bike helmet from slipping off her tiny head. Clearly, at six years old she knew it all.

"Well, I'm *Mallory's* mom and it's not okay for her! She's too young. Four is too young."

Baby Chloe started to cry. I wrapped her tightly in the towel, probably too tightly.

"But, Mommy, it's not fair. I don't like you, you're mean!"

For emphasis, she stomped her purple leopard-print plastic shoe on the hardwood floor and curled her small hands into fists, striking the air between us. Stomp, stomp, stomp, went the little foot. Punch, punch, punch, went the little fists. "You have to come outside *with* me," she said, crossing her arms and looking up at me defiantly while blinking back tears.

"I can't. I've already explained that to you. Daddy is out and I'm taking care of the baby. I have to dress her for bed and feed her."

I was jiggling Chloe on my hip to keep her from crying and rubbing my temples with my free hand to keep *myself* from crying.

"Then you're not my mother anymore!" she screamed, leaning forward with her hands stretched behind her back as if she might take off. In contrast with her behavior, her pageboy haircut, big brown eyes, and full pink lips made her look as sweet as Strawberry Shortcake.

> My kids make me crazy, but in many ways they also make me better.

This is when I snapped. It was sudden, as it always is. I forgot that I was talking to two children who couldn't read, let alone understand the concepts of pedophiles and hit-and-runs. I bent down and beckoned the two girls to come closer. I smiled demurely with a slight tilt of my head for emphasis and spoke softly: "Girls, what would you do if a car full of strangers pulled up and one of them had a gun?" I improvised the shape of a gun with my free hand. "Or a knife?" I made a cutting motion across my neck with my free hand. "What would you do then?"

They both look wide-eyed into our cul-de-sac with its manicured lawns and pristine, freshly painted homes. Welcome flags fluttered in the wind beneath trendy awnings and above fancy iron railings. The only strangers who ever drove down our street were house-hunting or lost. But they didn't know that.

"Well, okay then," the neighbor girl said and turned, no doubt excited to tell her mother about my breakdown.

"I guess we better close the door, Mommy," Mallory said quietly, her head lowered. "We don't want the strangers to come in."

"No, we don't, Baby," I said, pulling her into my hip and stroking her hair. "No, we don't."

. . . . . . . . . . . . .

As a television journalist, I capture some of life's most fantastic adventures and deepest tragedies. Over the wild ride of the past sixteen years, I might have thought I've seen it all. But it wasn't until I became a mother that the real life-learning started. I now see everything tempered through my children's eyes, including myself—and it's not always a pretty picture.

My kids make me crazy, but in many ways they also make me better.

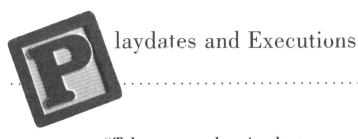

# laydates and Executions

"Do you sell the size 4 leotards in white or just pink?" I whisper into my cell as I hunch over in my seat in the back of the courtroom. "Well, I mean, don't you think a 6 would be too big? Or do they shrink?"

"Jury is coming back. Court is back in session. Order in the courtroom," the deputy's voice booms as everyone quickly shuffles back to their seats.

"Got to go," I say to the bewildered salesperson and shut the phone, trying not to make a loud *click*.

For Christ's sake, not again. Every time I get in the middle of something, it happens: The jury comes back with a verdict. I've got two days, *two days*, to find a white leotard for Mallory's ballet class. For some reason they have to wear frigging white this year, not pink, and wear their hair buns like girls out of a nineteenth-century painting. I don't know how to do a frigging bun (I can barely manage a ponytail), and I certainly don't have time to run all over town looking for a white leotard.

"Madame, do you have a unanimous verdict?" the judge asks the foreperson of the jury from his perch on the bench. His eyes peer over the wire-framed glasses teetering on the bridge of his nose. Nothing, I mean *nothing*, pisses off judges more than the sound of a cell phone ringing. I quickly double-check and make absolutely sure mine is on vibrate.

Sure enough, as the judge waits for the answer from the jury, my phone starts vibrating wildly in my hand like a live fish on the deck of a boat. I grab it just in time to keep it from slipping out of my hand onto the floor. A name comes up on the caller ID. It's the mother of one of Mallory's friends. We've been trying to connect for a week to set up a playdate, but I keep missing her calls because of more pressing issues, like a murder trial.

"Yes, your honor, we have a unanimous verdict," the foreperson says to the judge, her fingers shaking visibly as she hands the paper to the clerk. The clerk, in turn, hands the paper to the judge. After reading it, the judge hands it back to the clerk.

I've seen this a thousand times, but every time I'm still fascinated by the fact that a person's life is literally in the hands of twelve people, twelve *regular* people like you and me. I never tire of the human drama in the courtroom; the problem is that at the same time I often have my own human drama going on at home.

It takes every shred of resolve that I have not to answer the phone. Clearly, I can't do it now that court is back in session and a man's life is on the line. But my sanity is on *this* line. It's just one more call that I have to return. One more call that I have no time to return. One more call I will forget to return.

"The jury finds the defendant guilty of murder in the first degree," the clerk reads from her spot next to the judge's bench.

The courtroom erupts. There are tears of sadness from the defendant's family on one side of the room, and hugs and tears of joy from the victim's family on the other side of the room. Tripods click as photographers take their cameras down, and papers shuffle as reporters close their laptops and stuff everything into their briefcases for the mad dash into the hall.

It's what we in the business call a gang-bang. We chase everyone into the hallway and ambush them into doing interviews with us. For some reason the crowd mentality seems to actually encourage people to talk to us. It's like they feel like they don't have a choice.

My phone vibrates again. I wish I could be one of those people who just ignored it, just stuffed it into my bag and forgot about it, but I can't. It's a sickness. I *have* to know who is calling. This time I can see it's my daughters' doctor's office. The nurse is calling me to let me know if Mallory's strep culture is positive. Damn, I hope she leaves the message on my voice mail and doesn't make me call her back for the information. I'll never get through to her if I have to call her back. I'll be in Voice Mail Hell where no matter how hard you try you can never talk to a real human being. It's maddening.

But I can't worry about the strep test right now. After all, if she has it, she's already probably infected half her class. What good is it going to do to yank her out of class at this late hour?

The judge decides to take a break before sentencing. We jump up like the professionals we are and try to beat one another to the doorway. It's a very mature game that we play, especially in light of the human tragedy that the case represents. We're all hoping to get family members and lawyers on camera. Preferably, we want to interview someone from each camp on either side of the case. I reach into my jacket for my reporter's notebook and pull out a plastic horse and a lollipop. Wrong pocket. I finally locate the pad and . . . a Strawberry Shortcake pencil.

The gaggle of reporters and photographers is pushing in on the crying mother of the defendant, everyone jockeying for position. I drop to the floor on my knees in front of the woman, arching my back to keep the microphone high and near her face. She's sobbing. I'm thinking that my back is sore from pushing the baby jogger up the big hill from the park on Saturday afternoon. *Focus,* I tell myself, *focus.*

> I reach into my jacket for my reporter's notebook and pull out a plastic horse and a lollipop. Wrong pocket.

After the interview we make another mad dash down six flights of stairs to the street, where our live truck is waiting. I'm balancing my open computer on my forearm, carrying a pile of tapes in my hand, and swinging my briefcase behind me, hoping papers don't scatter, or worse yet, hoping I don't hit some poor old lady in the head.

I really want to get bottled water from the machine, but I have only four quarters, and two I'm saving for Mallory's United States coin collection. Don't ask me how we got into this. I'm not a collector. I actually abhor collections of any kind. But somehow I mentioned it to her one day that it would be cool to collect a quarter from each state, and now here I am dehydrating myself so that she can have her collection.

This is usually about the time my news desk calls, when I'm on deadline and can't spare a minute to pee, let alone answer a tedious question that would require a simple Google on their part.

But don't get me started on people who work in air-conditioned cubicles versus those of us who work in the real, sweaty world where eating and peeing can be luxuries on a busy day.

"Yeah, don't know the answer to that. I probably won't have time in the next twenty-seven minutes to find that out," I say, trying to catch my breath after navigating the stairs in too-high heels at high speed. "Hold on, I've got another call. I've got to take this," I say, clicking over. I'm greeted by Chloe's cherubic voice.

"Hi, Sweetie, how are you?" I say, immediately changing my tone from serious Lois Lane to a loving Doris Day. "I love you too! Did you have a good day? Did you go to time-out? Well, why did you hit him? That's not nice. Did you say you were sorry? Good. What about the potty? Did you go in the potty? Just one accident? Well, that's okay. Mommy's got to go. I'll see you at home, love you! Let me talk to Daddy."

Grif gets on the phone and I'm back to Lois Lane. "Hey, I'm on deadline, call you later."

Obviously I have my priorities straight, at least in my mind I do. I never decline a call from my girls, even on deadline, and I *always* make deadline.

By this time my news desk has hung up on the other line and I'm frantically tapping on my computer, trying to come up with a coherent script that can be edited and air in twenty-three minutes. As usual, I make it on the air with seconds to spare, and I never regret taking Chloe's call.

## LIKE MOTHER, LIKE DAUGHTER

I think most of us learn our work-life equilibrium from watching our parents. My mother returned to school, *law school,* when I was eleven. By the time I was a teenager, she was a practicing attorney working crazy hours and trying to keep herself from going crazy. Remember, this was the '80s. Women were allowed to work, but they still had to do everything at home, and they weren't allowed to complain about it. I learned a lot from watching my mother, a lot about what to do and what not to do.

One thing my mother did, and still does to this day, is to always take my call. I'm forty and let's just say she's in the latter part of her sixth decade. She is a very busy, successful divorce lawyer outside Philadelphia. But even when she's working, she's still a mother first. Even when my mother is with a client, her secretary puts me through.

"Hello, Amanda, I have someone with me, darling, but I have a minute," she says with her W.A.S.P. lockjaw working overtime. "What can I do for you?" Clearly, she's with a client. I feel bad for interrupting her. I wish her secretary had just told me she was with someone and had taken a message.

"Well, Mom, it's nothing, I'll call you later."

"No, no, go ahead. Marvin doesn't mind. Do you, Marvin?" she asks her client, who I'm sure is mortified that his attorney is sharing his name with her daughter.

"Well, I was wondering if you liked those black-and-white glasses on page 3 of the Pottery Barn catalog," I say, with hesitation. "I thought they might look good with my new dining room set."

The silence on the other end of the line is so deafening I think she might have hung up. That's when I hear Marvin cough and I realize that I'm on speakerphone.

· · · · · · · · · · · · · · · · · · · · · · · · · · · · · · · · · · · · · · ·

## "YOU ARE MY SUNSHINE"

I don't travel often for work, but when I do, it throws my entire family into a tailspin. I leave specific instructions for Grif about everything from the field trip at Chloe's day care to where he can find the already-packed bag for Mallory's sleepover. It's probably overkill. I could probably do a whole lot less preparation and the kids would still be alive when I got home. But I can't help myself. I wouldn't feel complete as a champion martyr if I didn't do *everything* before I left.

When I'm away, everyone pitches in to help Grif. Neighbors have him and the kids over for dinner, relatives offer to take the kids for the night. When a husband is out of town, no one worries about the wife left behind with the kids. Of course not, she can fend for herself. But if a man is left alone with the kids, watch out! Call the National Guard, fix some casseroles for him, start a prayer chain, because clearly he is going to need some help. Remember, folks, it takes a village to help a man care for children.

I call home to listen to my messages from the road and am greeted with a steady stream of voice mails from people who want to help. "Grif, I know you have your hands full this week. Let me know if there's something we can do to help, we're here for you." For some reason it's beyond comprehension that a man can handle all of the household and child-rearing duties by himself for a few days. Well, I'm here to tell you, my husband can not only handle it, he's pretty good at it. No need to raise the threat level to orange. He's going to be okay.

My connection with my kids while I'm working becomes even more critical when I travel. The cell phone is my lifeline, bridging me from my news world into every little detail of their daily lives. *Nothing* is too mundane to talk about.

"What did you have for lunch?" I ask Mallory.

"Peaches. Peaches and bread," she says matter-of-factly in her six-year-old way.

"That's it?" I ask, imagining her starving to death before I return.

"There was something called *bologna* on the bread. I don't like it. I gave it to Sierra," she says, bored with my line of questioning. I stumble over a pile of debris and barely miss sticking a rusty nail through the toe of my construction boot. I'm surrounded by leveled homes, piles of debris, tattered clothes, and curled photographs hanging from trees. I am in Mississippi in the aftermath of Hurricane Katrina.

"Well, what else did you do today? Who did you play with?" I ask, wondering why it's so impossible to elicit responses over the phone from a child who never shuts up at home.

"I don't know," she says. "I played with Abigail and I drew a picture of a rainbow and a zebra, that's it, that's all I can remember. Oh yeah, and I found some cool rocks we can paint."

I lean on the brick frame of a front porch that's still standing. The house is gone. "Well, that sounds like fun, I can't wait. Are you being good for Daddy?" I ask. Spray-painted on the house across the street from me is the number of people who lived in the house after the hurricane along with a big **X** and a date to show that the house has been searched for bodies.

"Yeah, I think so. Hold on. Daddy, am I being good?" she yells. He must say yes because she immediately responds. "Yes, except for when I hit Chloe in the head with the light saber, but it was an accident."

I'm not convinced, but I say, "I'm sure it was, Baby, I'm sure it was. I love you. Let me talk to your sister." I wonder where all the kids who lived in this destroyed neighborhood are now living. At my feet in a pile of pictures I see torn, water-stained class pictures of a boy who looks to be about Mallory's age.

"Okay, I love you too, Mommy. I miss you too. When are you coming home again?" She asks this every night.

"Soon, Baby, real soon," I say, not really knowing for sure myself. "Put Chloe on."

The only way I know that Chloe is on the phone is that I hear her heavy breathing. Even at three years old she has a habit of just listening but not responding. By the time she gets to the phone, she is usually sniffling because she has been crying and trying to grab the phone out of Mallory's hand. Mallory always gets to go first and that steams Chloe to no end. I'm sure this pattern will be repeated many times over in their lives.

"Hey, Baby," I say in my most soothing Mommy tone. "How are you?"

She breathes heavily into the receiver.

"I love you," I say in a singsong voice.

"Sunshine," she says in a muffled, high-pitched baby voice.

I know exactly what she's talking about. I look around to see if anyone is listening, which is ridiculous. I'm in a disaster zone. To my right is a tattered American flag that someone stuck on the top of a crumbling dresser. To my left is an impassable road with debris six feet deep. I'm alone.

*"You are my sunshine, my only sunshine. You make me happy when skies are gray. You'll never know, dear, how much I love you. Please don't take my sunshine away,"* I sing as I marvel at the juxtaposition of my surroundings and the tone of the song.

I have an awful voice, except in the shower and after a couple of drinks. Honestly, I suck. I love to listen to music. My husband is an accomplished musician who plays drums, piano, and the trumpet. I love to listen to him, but I can't carry a tune. But Chloe doesn't seem to notice or mind.

"Again, Mama, again," she says in her baby voice that I know she is quickly outgrowing. "Pleeeeeeeeeeeeease!"

And so for the next ten minutes I stand in the middle of what looks like the end of the world and I sing to the center of my world.

. . . . . . . . . . . . . . . . . . . . . . . . . . . . . . . . . . . . . . . . . . .

## MOMMY HAS NO MORE SICK DAYS

Traveling for work is an obvious hardship for families with young children, but keeping it together even when you *don't* travel is tough. There are days when I try to figure out what separates me from the crazy guy who gave me the finger in traffic on the way home from work, and I think *not much,* just exhaustion—I'm too tired to give him the finger back.

One of the hardest things about being a working parent is dealing with sick days. When I see the day care number come up on my caller ID on my cell phone, my hands start to shake. I panic because a call means one of my children is injured or sick. Now you might think I'm shaking because I love them so much just the thought of them being sick provokes an anxiety fit. But that's not *entirely* the case. Part of what provokes the anxiety is knowing someone is going to have to leave work early.

> Someone is going to have to leave work early.

"Well, how sick is she?" I ask the day-care teacher.

"She's throwing up and has a high fever."

"I mean, how high is high, and how many times has she thrown up?" I ask, fishing around for a way out of what I know is coming next.

"She needs to be picked up," the teacher says.

"Okay, okay," I say, resigned. Now, this is where the real negotiations begin: I dial Grif's number.

"Hi, it's me. Mallory is sick. Can you pick her up?"

Silence.

Finally, he says, "I've got a lot going on here. It's really not a good time."

"I've got a 6:00 live-shot downtown. It's the lead story. I can't do it," I say, gritting my teeth over the phone. This argument makes him madder than anything else. To him, it's tough luck—I've got a sick kid and the news will just have to do without me. But, sadly, my managers do not share his wisdom. Sometimes this is the moment when he reminds me that his income is *double* mine, that he puts food on the table and shoes on the baby.

I mean, I know I'm not transplanting a heart or flying an airplane, but being on the news is something, it's more important than other things I could be doing. Eventually, he sees it my way. Or at least he wisely gives in to avoid the my-job-is-more-important-than-your-job fight.

"Okay, I'll do it, but I absolutely can't take tomorrow off. If she's still sick, you have to do it. It's your turn," he says, leveraging his bargaining power to the hilt. Just before he clicks his cell phone shut, he says, "And if I'm picking her up, you make the doctor's appointment."

I, of course, am banking on her making a miraculous recovery, or at least masking her symptoms with medicine so that she can return to day care the next day. Otherwise, I'll deplete one more sick day from my dwindling stash.

Truth be told, Grif is a great father. He adores his daughters. He does more than the majority of married men I know.

But even in the twenty-first century, family responsibilities are not divided fifty-fifty and may never be. It's still 65 percent me and 35 percent him. Maybe the next generation of women will change this; maybe I'm raising the ones who will. *Maybe.*

· · · · · · · · · · · · · · · · · · · · · · · · · · · · · · · · · · · · · · ·

## BACKGROUNDING

No matter what your profession is, work does not end when you walk out the door at the end of the day. With the advent of e-mail,

> When my children are with me, they always demand my full attention, especially when I'm *not* giving it to them.

cell phones, and Blackberries, the work–personal life balance has become murky. There's no complete ending to one and beginning to the other. They mix together like leftovers in your grandmother's mystery stew. I can handle a certain amount of personal business concerning my children while I conduct business, but it's very hard to conduct business when I'm *with* my children.

In television we call people who walk in front of the camera on the street or in the newsroom in front of studio cameras backgrounders. Basically, they want to be on TV, but they don't really have an honest way to make that happen. So they wave, or make silly faces, or just stroll by and try to look cool.

My kids have decided they are going to be backgrounders on every work-related phone call that I receive on my days off. Anyone who calls can't help but notice and comment on their efforts.

"Oh, those must be your kids," says the spokesperson from the attorney general's office as Chloe whimpers in pain and Mallory laughs, having just kicked her sister in the head with her sneaker.

"Yes, yes, that's right," I say, swatting them both on the head lightly with my hand and making a shush sign with my finger up to my mouth as they try to climb out of the shopping cart. "So, anyway, you were saying about that death penalty case?"

Cue the screaming. Mallory pushes Chloe down in the cart and she bangs her head on the retractable seat that they both refuse to sit in.

"Mommy, she banged me," Chloe screams.

"Do you need to go?" the woman on the other end of the line says. "I mean, really, we can talk about this Monday."

"She pushed me first," Mallory barks, her arms crossed and lips pursed.

"No, no, I can talk," I say as I steer the cart into a shampoo display in the middle of the aisle. I'm determined for some sick reason to prove that I am a capable multitasker. The truth is that I'm really barely holding onto my sanity. I'm seconds away from hanging up the phone, throwing it into the Boston lettuce display, and pushing the shopping cart into the table of fresh blueberry muffins in front of me.

I can't talk, not now, not *ever*. When my children are with me, they always demand my full attention, especially when I'm *not* giving it to them. I know it's partly my fault for answering the call in the first place. When I'm at work and I see that day-care number pop up on the caller ID, I have to answer it. So when I'm with my kids and I see an important work call coming through, I feel like I have to answer it. But the truth is, I don't *have* to do anything. That's what caller ID is all about, *not* answering the phone. Maybe I'll try it someday.

. . . . . . . . . . . . . . . . . . . . . . . . . . . . . . . . . . . . . . . .

## WONDER WOMAN

Just before my twenty-year high school reunion, I started rummaging through my memorabilia. My mother allowed each of us to keep one box of sacred things from our youth. When I got my first house, she promptly mailed the box to me. Clearly the stuff was not so sacred to *her.*

When I was growing up, the deal was when the treasure box filled up we had to clean it out and make room for more. Her system, which actually seemed cruel at the time, I now see as brilliant. In her mind it was geared at keeping the clutter and junk in the house to a minimum. Looking back on this, I see I was forced to decide what was the most sacred. This is a choice, whether we know it or not, we are forced to make every day in our adult lives.

I couldn't figure out why I had, at one time, deemed my middle school yearbook sacred. Only when I really examined it and remembered that I was the managing editor did I realize why I had kept it, or at least I *thought* that was the reason. Then I found the real reason on page nineteen.

Our class had apparently come up with a list of what we planned to be in twenty years. Some of the answers were standard: teacher, doctor, scientist. Others were fanciful: astronaut, movie star, president. I scanned the list, looking for my name. There it was separated from my name by a dot-dot-dot, *Wonder Woman.* At twelve years old I had decided that I was not going to be something predictable, like a lawyer, but that I was destined to be a superhero.

I thought about this hard. Does Wonder Woman change diapers? Does she grocery shop at 10:00 at night with a button missing from her jacket and a coffee stain on her skirt after eating a candy bar for dinner? Does she screech to a stop at a red light when her daughter screams "You forgot my show-and-tell!" from the backseat? Does she make playdates and doctor's appointments, buy birthday presents and ballet leotards, sign valentines and sleep in a twin bed crammed up against the wall with a scared child? Does she? I don't think so. Wonder Woman has magic powers. She doesn't need to do any of this tedious stuff to be cool.

But if the definition of Wonder Woman is less about being a superhero with superpowers and more about being a super mother with above-average powers, well then maybe, just maybe, my prediction wasn't all that far off.

This year for Halloween Chloe has decided to be Wonder Woman the superhero, complete with the red, white, and blue bikini, the crown, the cape, the gold go-go boots, and those bracelets that repel bullets.

I wonder if it comes in my size.

# The Great Equalizer

*"A friend is one who knows all about you
and likes you anyway."*
—Christi Mary Warner

Mallory's first day of first grade started on a Friday, my day off. This seemed lucky for both of us because it meant I could stay with her at the bus stop until the bus came, and then meet her there at the end of the day. As with many firsts, the first day of school, the first day of first grade, the first time riding the bus, things do not always go well.

The bus was late, *very* late, late arriving in the morning and coming home. When Mallory still hadn't arrived close to an hour after school was dismissed, I made about thirty-seven phone calls to everyone from the principal to the school secretary to the school district's transportation department.

Meanwhile, my office calls wanting to know if a body of a woman missing for ten days had been found.

"Can you just call one of your sources?" an assignment editor in my newsroom asks me on my cell phone as I pace the corner looking for the big yellow school bus to come screaming around the corner. "I mean we're hearing chicken bones in a

Dumpster, but it could be her," he says, without a trace of humor in his voice.

"I'll do what I can," I say as I see the principal's name pop up on my caller ID on my other line. I quickly switch over. "Hi, Jim, do you know anything?" He tells me that the bus has just arrived at the school and the kids are boarding. She'll be home soon. Thank God. Just then a cop who I paged is beeping in on my caller ID. In the meantime, with my other hand, I'm trying to keep Chloe out of the busy street. "Danger, danger," I yell at her. "No, Jim, I'm sorry, not you, thanks for the update." The cop confirms the bones are in fact chicken bones. I scoop Chloe up in my free arm and call my office and tell them the news. But minutes later, just as the bus pulls up, the cop calls back to tell me the body has been found in another location.

> In a perfect world we could be good mothers and be good at our chosen profession and never feel guilty.

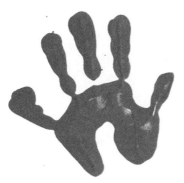

"They found the body," I say to my assignment editor as I see the bus pulling up to the curb. "I don't have the details." But of course he *wants* details. I've spent several hours waiting for a bus. I haven't had time to shower or put on makeup. Chloe is trying her best to wedge herself beneath the stairs of the bus, and he wants *details.*

I hug Mallory as she steps off the bus and then immediately begin dialing my source to see if I can get more details about the body before news time. As we walk down the street, the three of us holding hands, I have a cell phone planted to my ear, *and* I'm trying to listen to all the details of Mallory's first day of school.

In a perfect world we could be good mothers and be good at our chosen profession and never feel guilty. But it's not a perfect world, and as a result, you have to *play the game* when you're at the office.

The game is pretty simple, really. To your managers you are always 100 percent committed to any kooky idea they ever have, even if it means screwing up your family life. Then, at the last minute, you come up with an excuse as to why you can't do the kooky thing. But never, I repeat, *never* mention kids.

"Fly up to Maine in a C-130 military transport plane and cover an ice storm, absolutely, sounds like a great opportunity. Let me just check with my husband first," you say with the enthusiasm of a race horse that can't wait to get out of the gate.

And then you get back to them with something about a family reunion, or your dog is having surgery, *it really doesn't matter* as long as you don't invoke the Kid Clause. It's preferable to use any other excuse that you can think of just to avoid bringing your ovaries into the conversation.

The Kid Clause highlights every manager's underlying secret fear—that women of young children are unreliable because of their responsibilities at home. Forget about the fact that we are more efficient because time constraints force us to work smart. Forget about the fact that we are pros at organization because we not only manage our homes but also our families, and still manage to do a good job at work. And forget the fact that motherhood makes us more human, less entitled, less arrogant, and generally just better people all around. No, employers only see the dark side of the Kid Clause—maternity leave, sleepless nights, and sick days.

To me, mothers *are* superhuman with supernatural powers. Like experienced jugglers, they keep a dozen glass balls in the air at one time without breaking a single one.

"The key," my friend Lisa says, "is to let your boss think you're 100 percent into your job, you're a cheerleader, you're a team player, you can't get enough. It's all about pretending. Obviously your kids come first, but you can't tell your manager that."

You also can't just say, "I'll deal with that child-rearing thing after I finish this big project at work." If you do, you'll wake up one day and have a Goth girl who wears charcoal black eyeliner and a safety pin through her nose and writes suicide poetry.

If your job is more important to you than your kids, there's something very wrong with you—so wrong, in fact, that I can't imagine any employer wanting an employee of such bad character. Yet, if you are honest about your priority list to your employer—family first, job second—you won't go far in your career. Our mothers were the first generation of women who thought they could have it all. Our legacy is that we know we *can't* have it all.

But we keep on trying.

· · · · · · · · · · · · · · · · · · · · · · · · · · · · · · · · · · · · · · · · ·

## THE CLUB

One of the best perks of motherhood is membership in "the club." It's a secret club, the motherhood club, so secret, in fact, you don't know that you're not a member until you become one. Suddenly, women you would never normally speak to, or who would never normally speak to you, become your allies. It doesn't matter if you have nothing in common; once you are responsible for a small human being, you have an automatic lifetime membership with all the joys and heartaches it includes, free of charge.

The club allows you certain privileges. You can talk to strangers in the grocery store, at the mall, or in line at the movies if they also have children with them. There's an understanding between booger-wiping, shoe-tying, boo-boo-soothing women that transcends all potential differences.

Take Belinda, a bank teller at one of the branches I occasionally pop into during my workday. Her desk is covered with portraits of her daughter. Artwork complete with glitter, paper cutouts, and various sizes of handprints are taped to the inside of her cubicle. The corners of the colored construction paper pieces have faded and curled from the sunlight streaming in from the drive-through teller window behind her. Belinda's husband drives a crane, they live in a double-wide, and she wears Christmas sweaters. But the differences melt away when we talk.

"He comes home and plops down on the couch, starts channel surfing," Belinda says through gritted teeth. "I'm like, do you not see the piles of laundry, do you not see the unmade beds, do you not know there's homework to be done, dinner to be made, a dishwasher to unload? I work, too—what's he thinking?"

"He's not thinking, that's the problem," I say. "Men are like day laborers that construction companies pick up on the corner every morning. If you tell them exactly what to do and promise them a beer afterwards, they can be hard workers. But they're not going to get off that corner or that couch without a good swift kick, if you know what I mean."

Belinda nods fervently.

"I like to look at myself as the manager and he's my employee," I say. "I like to make him think he has choices, like a child. But doing nothing is not an option. I say things like, do you want to give the girls a bath or clean the kitchen? Or, do you want to put the girls to bed or do the laundry?"

"They're just not like us," Belinda says, grinning and shaking her head. "Not wired like us, not at all."

"Amen, sista," I reply. "You can say that again."

· · · · · · · · · · · · · · · · · · · · · · · · · · · · · · · · · · · · · · ·

## GAME ON

The only problem I have with women like me is the sense of competition. After all, we're intense at the office—why wouldn't we be intense in how we parent? If little Max is reading at a second-grade level, by God, Mallory should be, too. Keeping up with the Joneses is a major issue in child development—from when your children walk, to when they potty train, to whether or not they win the Nobel Peace Prize.

"So Mallory is in the gifted class?" another little girl's mother asks me. "For some reason Katie didn't get picked for that. That's odd."

"Yeah, but you know how it is, they just pick the kids who raise their hands a lot," I say, trying to downplay it but secretly thinking that my child is brilliant. What mother doesn't think that?

"And what about Chloe, is she fully potty trained yet?" she probes, knowing this is my weak spot. "George has been potty trained since he was just two. No accidents, isn't that amazing?"

"Well, for the most part she is, but she's still wearing a Pull-Up at night," I say, knowing that she has just gotten in a subversive strike.

Believe it or not, this is an area where I have learned to be diplomatic, a rare feat for me. We *all* think our kids are great. I'm no exception, but I don't feel the need to prove my kid is better than someone else's kid, especially when it comes to my friends' children. I let them talk about their children, and I listen. When I talk about mine, I try not to brag too much.

If we were being brutally honest, I might say, "I guess Chloe is a little behind on the potty-training curve, especially behind George. He's onto something."

And she might say, "Oh, well, I guess Mallory is smarter than Katie."

Then we'd hug and go get a raspberry martini. But somehow I don't think this is ever going to happen, not when we live in a culture where *American Idol* and *The Amazing Race* set the bar for how we compete with one another.

## GUILT ME ONE MORE TIME

Working mothers constantly talk about how guilty they feel. It's okay to feel that way and to acknowledge it among other working women. But if a nonworking mother makes you feel guilty, things can get ugly.

"Can you believe she made me feel guilty for not coming to the preschool tea party?" my friend Melanie says about a mother at her child's school. "I mean I went to the Halloween party, that stupid holiday thing, I even made heart cookies for the frigging Valentine's thingy for God sakes! I mean, what's her problem? She's sitting home watching *Oprah* and looking up recipes for pot roast while I'm slaving away here at the office for ten hours—what doesn't she get?"

Clearly, there's a lot that women on both sides of the fence don't get. I don't understand how someone could stay home with kids all day long and not get bored. They don't understand how I can be away from my kids all day and not feel guilty. The truth is sometimes stay-at-home moms do get bored and sometimes I do feel guilty. And I don't just feel guilty for being away from my girls; I feel guilty for being away from them and being happy about it, the kind of happiness that freedom inspires.

**The truth is sometimes stay-at-home moms do get bored and sometimes I do feel guilty.**

The key to a healthy friendship between mothers who do work and mothers who don't work is being brutally honest about the negatives that come with each choice.

I have a lot of friends who are mothers who don't work. Most of them used to work and then chose to stay home with their children. These moms are keenly aware of the challenges and benefits of either choice. Having friends in both camps keeps me grounded and allows me to see the world from multiple points of view.

Take my best friend Amy. She used to be a television reporter. We went to graduate school together and roomed together early on in our fledgling careers when our lives were more colorful. In the early '90s we lived in dumpy, subsidized housing with my hippie, stoner boyfriend who came for a night and never left. Finally, we were forced to give him a key and charge him rent. He made candles and tie-dyes and drove a VW van. Two years later when I left for greener pastures, I let him keep everything in the apartment—the futon, beanbag chairs, the television with the hanger for an antenna. I was done.

Amy eventually went into politics and became a public relations honcho for a top state official. But when she got married and had children, she decided to stay home. In my opinion, it was a brave decision. Amy is a brilliant woman, a great writer, and has a lot to offer the business world, but she has even more to offer her children. She's the kind of mother who gets down on the floor and builds things or plays with glitter glue with her kids. The last time I was on the floor, I was looking for my heels that someone kicked under the couch. As for glitter glue, it's simply not allowed in my house.

Amy reads the news online every day, watches the news on television, reads books, and keeps her brain sharp. But she also volunteers in the classroom at school, goes to soccer practice, and organizes playgroups for the kids.

Amy and I often talk about the divergent roads we have taken. She says she couldn't do what I do, and I tell her I couldn't do what she does. We both mean it. To our credit, I think our history, and our friendship, have outlasted these dramatic changes in our lives.

The other day I got a message from Amy on my cell phone.

"Hey, just returning your call," I say. "What's up?"

"Where are you? It's so loud, I can hardly hear you," she says.

"I'm in the helicopter, we're just flying over a forest fire in Virginia."

"Thanks for reminding me how boring my life is," she says with a laugh, "I'm knee-deep in poop right now."

"Got it, do you need to go?" I ask.

"No, no, do you?"

"No, I'm cool, I've got six minutes until the show," I say. "Tell me about your day."

The truth is that women are connected by motherhood in a way that nothing else binds us. Whether we work, don't work, are poor, rich, black, white, old, young, we're experiencing something so wonderfully frustrating that we can't help but share it with others. It's what we in journalism call "a universal truth." It's common ground, an island that we can all float on when there's nothing else but a murky cesspool of chaos all around it.

# ipping It in the Bud

*"Behind every great man there is a surprised woman."*
—Maryon Pearson

Some people see the vasectomy as the end of the parenting journey. I see it as the beginning. This is the point when you truly realize that you are not just having babies, you are raising children. But who thinks about what comes next? I certainly didn't. In the real world it goes marriage, kids, and then the vasectomy.

You can see them at the grocery store, at parties, at the office. They are geldings, no longer able to procreate needy human beings who cost a fortune to raise. I think this is the reason men agree to vasectomies. For them everything comes down to cost. Let's face it, kids cost money; the more kids you have, the more you pay. After two kids, most men are done.

My husband decided it was time to take the big step the first night we came home from the hospital with our second child, Chloe. In fact, I think he called the urologist on the cell phone on the way home from the hospital and left a message. I'm not sure if it was the baby's screaming, Mallory's whining, or my crying that pushed him to make the call. I think he even had to call information to get the number, which is a big deal for him because it costs fifty cents.

Mallory was three and a half at the time, and to say she was having an adjustment problem would be like saying Hezbollah has anger issues. She put a blanket over Chloe's face and then bit her on the elbow. But it wasn't the danger that got to Grif; it was the tandem screaming. The baby cried because she was hungry, and because that's just what babies do. Mallory cried because her world had been rocked by a category 5 hurricane named Chloe cleverly disguised in a pink fleece blanket. I just cried.

> To say she was having an adjustment problem would be like saying Hezbollah has anger issues.

The very next day, unprompted, Grif called the urologist again and this time talked to a real live person and made an appointment for a consultation. This is a man who faints when he gives blood and who closes his eyes when he gets a shot. This is a man who wasn't sure he could be present for the birth of his children because of his aversion to pain, *other people's* pain. Yet he had decided it was time to nip Mother Nature in the bud, literally. At thirty-seven years old with a newborn baby, a toddler, and a full-time job, I had no energy to argue with his reasoning. Only later did I realize that a vasectomy gives a man license to have sex with *other* women, too, without fear of getting them pregnant.

· · · · · · · · · · · · · · · · · · · · · · · · · · · · · · · · · · · · · · · · · · · · ·

## THE CONSULTATION

The consultation involved us reading and signing a plethora of paperwork with the same phrase written in different ways over and over: "Are you absolutely, positively sure that you don't ever in your lifetime want to have another child?"

Not only did we have to answer the question on paper, but we also had to answer it in person. I imagined they did this to protect themselves from lawsuits, but for the life of me, I couldn't figure out on what grounds anyone could or would sue.

"Your honor, I submit to the court that my client didn't understand when she was asked twenty-seven times whether or not she was sure she didn't want more children what that meant," my lawyer would plead to the court after the vasectomy.

"Was she under the influence of drugs or alcohol?" the judge would ask.

"No, clearly, she's just not very bright, your honor," my lawyer would reply.

We signed the paperwork eagerly, almost too eagerly, and set up the appointment for the big day. Grif was nervous, but I took secret pleasure in the fact that after having two children, he would have to undergo an uncomfortable medical procedure. There is still no comparison to nine months of pregnancy followed by childbirth and breastfeeding, but I felt as if it was the least he could do.

· · · · · · · · · · · · · · · · · · · · · · · · · · · · · · · · · · · · · · ·

## TWENTY TIMES

It wasn't until I started talking to my girlfriends that I learned the specifics about what we were about to go through. Not only did I find out more men were in the vasectomy club than I realized but also that many people have a wealth of knowledge about vasectomies they are dying to share.

"You know about the twenty times, right?" my friend Tina said one day with a little tilt of her head and a smirk.

"No, twenty times . . . what do you mean?" I was in a perpetual no-sleep fog; sex was not at the top of my mind in between breastfeeding and taking care of a three-year-old.

"You know, he has to, you know, do it twenty times before it's safe, before you can be sure he's sterile. Then you go back to the doctor and get tested," Tina said, flipping both her hair and the pages of one of my magazines. "You've got to do it right or you could have a vasectomy baby. Don't forget Millie and Craig; little Robert was never supposed to be here," Tina nodded her head knowingly.

*Twenty times*, I thought, that's crazy talk. I started calculating how long it would take for us to have sex twenty times—a couple weeks, a couple months, a year? Then I started calculating how much the vasectomy would cost versus other forms of birth control and really wondered if it would pay for itself over my lifetime.

I pictured the nurses pulling out our dusty file, gathering around in a circle in the break room with their coffee, and having a good laugh. "They're still not back yet. Been eight months. Seems like that vasectomy was sure a big waste of time and money!" a nurse would cackle. "Anyone want to take bets we don't see them back before Christmas? Come on, anyone in?"

The pressure of the twenty times hung over my head like a black cloud. It meant that my husband would also have to come clean about masturbating. Otherwise, it would take that much longer. I knew he occasionally did it—all men do. But I didn't know if he would be comfortable sharing this information with me. Frankly, I wasn't sure that I really wanted to know all of his dirty little secrets.

"Oh, honey, add another one to the list," he would say. "I did it today in the bathroom on my lunch break. I had a few minutes, you know, and thought, what the heck, let's make it to number six!"

It never occurred to me to evaluate my sex life in such black-and-white terms. I decided the only way to handle it was to really step up my game after I got over the I-have-a-newborn-baby-don't-touch-me period. Clearly, after-the-vasectomy sex was going to have to become a priority if I was ever going to make it to twenty.

. . . . . . . . . . . . . . . . . . . . . . . . . . . . . . . . . . . . . . . . .

## THE BIG DAY

There wasn't a whole lot of preparation involved in getting ready for the main event. Well, there was one important thing—the shaving of the balls. The nurses gave us a handout complete with a diagram to walk you through the potentially hazardous activity. It said that if you had trouble doing it at home, the nurses would handle it on operation day.

I asked my husband if he wanted me to do it for him. After all, as a woman I know how hard it is to shave your bikini line. I couldn't imagine shaving a round area on your own body that you could barely see. I knew it would be a delicate process, but I was ready to take it on. To my complete surprise, my husband said he did not trust me to shave his balls. I found this interesting considering he trusted me to do just about anything else with them. Apparently, he didn't trust the nurses either. So he locked himself in the bathroom armed with a razor and a can of shaving cream. Twenty minutes later, he was bald.

> To my complete surprise, my husband said he did not trust me to shave his balls.

We dropped off Mallory at day care and headed to the doctor's office with baby Chloe, who was just a few weeks old at the time. Since the procedure was not expected to take long, I had planned to wait in the lobby. Grif was nervous. As I've said, he is not a trooper when it comes to medical procedures. Pain is not his thing. But as the breastfeeding mother of a newborn baby, I wasn't all that concerned with his anxiety. After all, I had pushed what felt like two elephants through what felt like the eye of a needle; he could get fixed.

"Good luck," I smiled at him, looking up from my magazine, the baby happily snoozing in my Baby Bjorn carrier.

He looked skeptical.

"You'll be fine," I said, patting him on the back and thinking about getting back to the article on romantic mountain spa getaways that had caught my eye. "Seriously, it's no big deal. Men do this all the time. How many bad stories have you heard about it?"

"Honestly, a lot," he said. "Remember Marty? He had serious pain, serious pain." He wrung his hands and looked down at the floor, shaking his head. "I think he had to go back in and get it tweaked or something."

"Okay, so one bad story. One out of how many, a dozen? You won't be that one," I said, looking at a photo of a woman getting a pedicure poolside surrounded by mountains, with a glass of champagne in her hand. "Look, it's totally up to you. You don't have to do it if you don't want to. It's your decision."

I closed the magazine and tried to make eye contact with him as he paced in front of me. I was getting slightly annoyed. The baby was due to wake up and feed any minute. I just wanted a little peace.

"Griffin!" the nurse yelled across the waiting room full of nervous men.

"What if I am? The one, I mean," he said as he walked slowly toward the open door where a rather large Hungarian-looking nurse was waiting, tapping her red pen on the edge of a clipboard. It reminded me of a *Saturday Night Live* skit—this was not a woman you wanted anywhere near your private parts with a sharp object. I stifled a giggle.

He looked back at me and I waved. Looking like a soldier in an old war movie heading off for his tour of duty, he bucked up, straightening his shoulders, and bravely disappeared behind the door.

I looked around the waiting room. It was obvious who was there for what. The room was divided into two categories: old men with kidney and bladder issues, and young men getting vasectomies. The young men tried not to meet one another's eyes. Maybe they were afraid they would talk each other out of it if they got the chance.

"Man, you don't want to get fixed? Neither do I," one would say to another. "The old lady is making me do it. Too much trouble for her to remember to take a frigging pill every day. Let's blow this thing off and get a burger and a beer."

. . . . . . . . . . . . . . . . . . . . . . . . . . . . . . . . . . . . . . . .

## THE SCROTUM HOLDER

Chloe finally woke up, crying uncontrollably. I tried to feed her a bottle of expressed breast milk, but she wouldn't take it. I jostled her on my shoulder, pacing up and down as the old men looked at me, annoyed. They had been there, done that, and had no tolerance for crying babies. The young men looked at me as walking confirmation that they were making the right choice.

It occurred to me that I could make some extra money handing out fliers for discount vasectomies on a street corner as I bounced a crying baby on my shoulder.

The Hungarian-looking nurse came out and whispered in my ear, "Did you bring a scrotum holder for your husband?"

"A what?"

"A scrotum holder, to hold everything in place after the op-

I was a woman on a mission: I had a hungry baby strapped to my chest and a husband who needed his scrotum held.

eration," she looked at me disapprovingly, tapping her red pen on the damn clipboard. I obviously had not read the operation checklist thoroughly.

"Oh, you mean an athletic supporter?"

"Well, yes, sort of. But it really is more specific than that. It's called a scrotum holder," she said, letting the phrase roll off her tongue with creepy emphasis on the word *holder*. "We can't let him leave without it. It's our policy."

I could feel the sting of redness spreading across my cheeks as the old men who overheard our conversation had perked up and were now looking directly at me.

I imagined a man leaving the building without a scrotum holder and his testicle falling off in the parking lot, rolling beneath a car. The wife would have to hand him the baby. She would be down on her hands and knees with a coat hanger trying to fish it out. "Hold on, I think I can get it. There's a darn oil slick under here that I'm trying to avoid. Wait, wait, I got it! Do you think the doctor can sew it back on?"

"No, I didn't bring one," I said to Nurse Olga. "No, but do I have time to run and get one?"

"Sure, just hurry back. When he's done he'll want to go home and sleep, I'm sure," she smiled a we've-got-to-take-care-of-our-man smile.

I had no idea where to get a scrotum holder. I really had no idea what a scrotum holder *was*. And I certainly wasn't about to utter the phrase to anyone in a store. So I ran to a local sporting goods store. I told the sixteen-year-old female cashier I was looking for an athletic supporter. I had no time to waste and tried not to be too concerned with being embarrassed, so I told her what it was for. I was a woman on a mission: I had a hungry baby strapped to my chest and a husband who needed his scrotum held. She blushed, the kind of red, splotchy blush that starts at the base of your neck and creeps up into your face in just seconds. She excused herself and went to look for the manager who "might know more about this kind of thing."

The manager ushered me to a rack of athletic supporters. Who knew there were so many different kinds? He saw me eyeing one and tapped me on the shoulder.

"Pardon me, but I don't think he'll need a cup. He doesn't need that much protection," he said, trying to control the twitching grin at the corner of his mouth.

I nodded, moving quickly beyond my mistake, and selected your basic run-of-the-mill jockstrap. Luckily, they are sized using a man's waist measurements. I didn't have to guess. I bought two just to be on the safe side and rushed back to the doctor's office.

## DISCHARGE

When I returned, they brought me back into the recovery room to talk about what kind of care my husband would need over the weekend. From what they were saying, it sounded like he needed a live-in maid-cook-nurse, a job I was totally unqualified for, especially in my present stage of life. But I smiled and nodded, acting like a little Tammy Wynette, standing by my man.

When I retrieved the jockstraps from the bag to hand them to Nurse Olga, the mood in the room changed dramatically. She glared at me. Clearly, the game was up. She realized I was not going to take care of my man at all, not like Tammy would.

"These are not *scrotum holders,*" she growled, again giving the phrase queer emphasis. "This will not work. He can't leave in this.

She held up the sad little jockstrap and swung it before my eyes like a pendulum, dangerously close to my personal-space bubble. For a moment I thought she might swing it in a full circle in the air on the edge of her finger and break into song, maybe a few bars of Gloria Gaynor's "I Will Survive."

"Well, I'm sorry," I said, feeling exasperated. "I guess you need to tell me where I can get one then."

She handed me a list of drugstores where I could find the mysterious and elusive scrotum holder. This would have been nice to have on my first journey. Nurse Olga told me I needed to recline the passenger seat so Grif could lie down in the car until I could get something to hold his scrotum in place. (Funny—I don't remember reclining in the car after having a baby.)

She also gave me a list of instructions for returning to get his sperm tested. There it was in black and white, and unlike the scrotum holder, I was ready for this part: "*The patient must have twenty ejaculations prior to returning to have his sperm tested.* During that time the couple should use another form of birth control. Not until you have two clean tests should you forgo birth control."

They also gave me two little plastic cups to collect the samples in. The fine print said they would accept samples only weekday mornings between 9:00 a.m. and 1:00 p.m. The sample could be no more than three hours old. I mulled this over. As a working mom with two children, mornings were a little too busy to fit in a hand-job between coffee and diapers. I decided he would be on his own with this one.

As I signed the sheet to show that I had read and understood it, I couldn't help myself. I laughed out loud and said, "Wow, twenty times. We'll see you in about five years!" The nurses at the desk just stared at me, not responding to my vasectomy humor in any way. I guess they had become jaded by hearing too many bad semen jokes over the years.

· · · · · · · · · · · · · · · · · · · · · · · · · · · · · · · · · · · · · · ·

## FURTHER HUMILIATION

Our first stop was a big chain drugstore. They had everything from tampons to digital cameras; surely they would have a scrotum holder. This time I got over my anxiety and used the proper term, as instructed by the nurse. I stopped short, however, of letting the phrase roll off my tongue seductively like the name of a pornographic movie. That was Olga's gig, not mine.

"Pardon me," I said to the two teenaged clerks at the pharmacy, a boy and a girl. "Do you have scrotum holders?" I asked, trying to sound clinical. The girl covered her mouth with one hand and put her other arm across her stomach as she doubled over in laughter. The boy made a loud snorting noise as he sucked a giggle back down his throat and steadied himself on the counter with both hands.

I remained unflustered. Remember, I was a woman on a mission. Nothing was going to get in my way, especially not some skinny, pimply teenagers having a good laugh at my expense. I explained in a calm tone exactly what I needed this item for and asked them to please help me as I had a baby in the car and a husband who had just undergone a vasectomy.

Clearly, it was the word *vasectomy* that sent them over the edge. The boy now exhaled his laughter and turned away from me. The girl covered her mouth with both hands, and it looked like she might even be crying.

Finally, they composed themselves and pitied me enough to give me a list of some specialty drugstores I might call.

"Excuse me, I'm looking for a scrotum holder," I would whisper into my cell phone, without a hint of humor in my voice. "Do you happen to have one?"

I said it over, and over, and over again, ignoring the muffled laughter from the pharmacy employees listening to my conversation, who were apparently now fascinated by my situation. Get over it already, I wanted to say. But instead I just glanced at them like a disapproving parent who might tell their parents they had been smoking behind the school.

I located one in a mom-and-pop drugstore on the other side of town that, according to the girl who answered the phone, had a variety of scrotum holders. Who knew about this racket? I hurried out, gratuitously thanking the clerks, who were still recovering from their laughing fit.

When I got to the car, Grif was reclined in the seat, stroking Chloe's hand as she screamed in the car seat behind him. It was going to be a long weekend.

## WHAT SIZE IS YOUR SCROTUM?

When I got to the mom-and-pop store, I was finally immune to any difficulty in saying *scrotum holder*. It now rolled off my tongue in a mundane way as if I were saying *cheese pizza*. In fact, I kind of liked the way it sounded. I practiced saying it in different ways, emphasizing a new syllable each time with a variety of inflections. Confident, I went right to the cashier: "Can you tell me where your scrotum holders are?" It was as if I were saying, "Excuse me, but where is your cough medicine?" I was that casual.

This time the girl's face behind the counter was impassive. She was obviously someone who had been asked the question before. Unlike her peers at the chain store, she knew what a scrotum holder was for, that it was serious business, not something to be taken lightly. I was impressed with her maturity.

I wondered if the store owner prepped his cashiers on this sort of stuff before he hired them. "Now you know people might ask about potentially embarrassing products, products like adult diapers, tampons, and scrotum holders. Can you handle that? Can you keep a straight face? Because if you can't, there's the door!"

"They're over there along that wall," she pointed lethargically, as if she directed people to the wall a thousand times a day. "If you have any questions, Al can help you." She pointed at a slight man preparing prescriptions at the end of the counter.

When I got to the wall, I saw that the packages were clearly labeled as scrotum holders. These were not jockstraps, not athletic supporters, but scrotum holders. *Yes, Virginia, there is such a thing as a scrotum holder,* I thought. They do exist. It took me a minute to get over the epiphany. Talk about a niche market. I only wish I had thought of it.

Here's the rub. Scrotum holders come in small, medium, large, and extra-large. The problem—the sizes are not based on waist size like the jockstraps but on actual scrotum size. This immediately presented an issue. I don't even have my husband's Social Security number memorized; I surely don't know the size of his scrotum.

I called on Al for his expertise in this area.

"Al, can I ask you a question? How do you know what size to get your husband?" I looked at him with pleading eyes, praying he wasn't going to send me to the car with a tape measure.

His red vest had his name embroidered in blue letters on the left side. He adjusted his wire-framed glasses on his thin nose. "Well, Miss," he said in a completely monotone voice, "the size is based on the circumference of the man's scrotum. Since most women don't have this number handy, I suggest you get a large one so as not to offend your husband."

It was clear he had said this to a million women before me. Al was no scrotum-holder-selling virgin. We stood there looking at each other in awkward silence. He adjusted his glasses again, pressing them against his temples. He didn't blink.

"Well then," he said, expressionless, "let me know if there's anything else I can do." He turned on his heels and headed to the back of the pharmacy, his red vest moving in sync with his stiff gait. I was left alone with the wall of scrotum holders.

I considered reality, and then I considered perception. I did what any smart woman would do in my situation. I bought the Large.

# HOMECOMING

When we returned home, Grif tried on the large scrotum holder. It looked like an oversize hammock holding a golf ball. But for now it would have to do.

I snickered a little at my mistake, but luckily he didn't notice. He promptly went to bed. I understood his need to rest directly after the surgery, but there he stayed for three days. The doctor told him to take it easy, lie down as much as possible, no lifting, no operating heavy machinery, all the usual stuff. But Grif took it a step further. He acted as if he had just had a heart transplant. He expected to be waited on. Of course, I had loads of time and energy to do that considering I was caring for a newborn baby and a toddler. Luckily, I didn't have enough energy to be angry about it.

It amazes me that after giving birth, women are expected to hop to it. After what can be the most painful and exhausting experience of your life, you begin breastfeeding (which can be equally painful and exhausting) and sleeping in two-hour shifts like a POW. There's no recovery time, period. But a man has a little procedure like a vasectomy and he's down for the count. He can barely lift a finger to change the channel on the remote.

I think it's more than just about having babies. We wax our bikini line and our eyebrows. We go to work when we have a fever and are throwing up rather than spare a sick day. We exercise until it hurts. Let's face it: Women have a higher threshold for pain.

When my mother-in-law found out my husband was having a vasectomy, she said, "I think when a man goes through this you should really treat him special that weekend and really take care of him." Remember, I was not sleeping much, taking care of two kids . . . and I get *this* advice. It sent me through the roof. I didn't get special treatment after having either baby, and I was about to shower him with the same. Clearly, I was going to take care of him. But cater to his every whim? No.

My mother always said: "Why start traditions you don't intend to keep?"

. . . . . . . . . . . . . . . . . . . . . . . . . . . . . . . . . . . . . . . . . .

## BACK IN THE SADDLE

Before long, the patient was up and around again. It would still be several weeks before we could have sex. To tell you the truth, I can't remember how long we had to wait. I do know that, not unlike a woman who has recently given birth, my husband was not eager to try the gear out anytime soon. He was afraid of potential pain and, even more importantly, he was afraid things wouldn't work correctly, playing into every man's greatest fear—that a vasectomy was really akin to castration. I assured him that everything would work just fine. I figured men wouldn't do it in such numbers if there was even a slight chance of permanent impotence. But, then again, I am not a doctor. What do I really know? There was probably something in the fine print on the documents we signed about impotence, right alongside the are-you-really-positively-sure-you're-done-wanting-children part.

We finally did it, tentatively. It reminded me of that old song "It Feels Like the First Time."

From there we had the daunting task of deciding how to handle (pardon the pun) the other nineteen ejaculations required to get cleared by the infertility police, namely Nurse Olga. We mutually decided to do it right. There had to be a list. I come from a long line of list makers and felt this was the only way to be sure.

I hung the list on the door inside my linen closet in between the bathroom and the bedroom. It needed to be in a convenient location where we would remember to check it off. At first we were vigilant about keeping track, and then things got murky.

I would look at the list after a few days of no activity and say, "Anything you want to tell me about this week, any masturbation in the shower?" The list forced us to confront the ugly truth that married men have a lot of sex alone. At first he resisted telling me. Then he realized that the only way we would reach our goal would be through honesty, no matter how awkward it was. After my scrotum holder experience, nothing could ruffle me.

Eventually, when we were at about sixteen, he said, "Let's just get the test. We're close enough. I'm sure I'm sterile."

I took this to mean that there were really four more times that he hadn't told me about.

"They said twenty, Grif, not sixteen," I said sternly. I'm very type A and wanted to make sure we were doing this right. Once again I imagined the nurses periodically pulling out our chart and chuckling over our dull sex life. "Anyone want to bet on when we'll see them again?" one would say. "I'd say at least three more months at the rate they're going," another would chime in.

About three months later I was cleaning out a closet and found the specimen jars that Grif was supposed to use to bring in his semen samples. I decided I would put them in the bathroom next to his sink to remind him that it was time to go ahead and get this thing over with. They sat there for about ten days. Every day I would call him at the office and remind him.

"How about that test?" I would ask with growing frustration in my voice. "You going to get that test?"

"Yeah, yeah, I'll get to it, been busy," he said. I could practically hear the shuffling of feet over the phone.

I didn't know if he would do it at the office. I pictured him locking his office door, telling his secretary to hold his calls, and going at it. Then I thought maybe he would do it at the doctor's office. I figured they were well-equipped to handle this sort of thing with private rooms and soft-porn magazines.

Finally he called me one day from work and simply said two words: "It's done."

I immediately knew what he was talking about. I didn't ask him how he accomplished the task. I didn't want to know. We exchanged a moment of silence over the phone. I was relieved and, unpredictably, a little sad.

It was a couple days before we could get the official results of the test. Neither of us expected anything else but a report that he was sterile. But we did have friends whose vasectomies didn't take, so we wanted to be cautious. I think he mentioned it to me one day in a list of things like: "Can you pick the kids up? We need milk, don't we? By the way, the doctor called, I'm sterile."

I didn't expect it to hit me the way it did. I thought I would be thrilled that all of the stuff we went through was worth it. It worked. I had always just wanted two kids. So did my husband. There was never any question about this. But all of a sudden a door was closing, a door that we as women are never quite sure we're ready to close.

. . . . . . . . . . . . .

About two months after the operation, Grif ran into the surgeon in Wal-Mart. Grif tugged on my sleeve and tried to catch the man's eye. "There he is," he said, as if he was a child spotting his homeroom teacher, "that's Dr. V. You know, the doctor who performed the operation." The doctor raised his hand slightly in an obligatory gesture and made a half-smile, the smile of a man who didn't recognize the person who was greeting him. At that moment Grif's face fell. I could almost hear the wind draining out of his sails. He couldn't believe that a man who had handled his scrotum didn't recognize him.

"Sorry, Sweetie," I said, "I guess it wasn't that good for him."

# weet Dreams and Sleep Machines

*"No matter how big or soft or warm your bed is,
you still have to get out of it."*
—Grace Slick

"Bzzzzzzzzzzz," the white noise machine hums next to my bed.

"Whoosh, whoosh, whoosh," goes the sleep-apnea machine attached to Grif's face.

"Waaaaaaaaaaaah," whines the baby monitor, which is on high so that it can be heard above the other machinery. Yet I continue to ignore it unless Chloe is in full-throttle mode.

This is not a laboratory, this is my bedroom. It's a place where no one in his or her right mind would want to sleep. It's a place where one loud annoying sound begets another. It's a well-orchestrated cacophony of noise that must meet a precise balance for everyone to sleep soundly and wake up alive. I sleep so far from Grif in our king-size bed to distance myself from his snoring that a family of four could easily pitch a tent between us.

One of the best-kept secrets about parenting is that you never have a good night's sleep again, period. Before you become a parent, no one tells you this, not in so many words. If they did, the world would be grossly underpopulated.

"How's the baby sleeping?" is one of the first questions we ask new parents. Why? Because it's a little jab, a little joke if you will, among parents who know that the days of sleeping, really sleeping, are long gone.

I'm a high-energy person, but I have my basic needs. Sleep is one of them. Before I had kids I considered sleeping a sport. I didn't get to do it nearly enough, but when I did do it, I was good at it, very good.

My husband and I bought black curtains for our room to make it cavelike. We purchased the best sheets, the softest blanket, and of course, the most comfortable mattress. We often talk about how much we love our bed, especially after we return from sleeping on a lumpy mattress with no back support in a hotel.

On weekends we used to turn the ringer off on the phone and have marathon sleep sessions. Sometimes on Sunday afternoons we'd go back to bed after brunch and end up sleeping for most of the day. I tried to convince myself that I was just catching up on missed sleep from the week, but in reality, I just couldn't get enough of it. It was intoxicating, like a drug. I was addicted. In retrospect I think my body knew that later on in life I would be gravely deprived of sleep.

As a teenager I would sleep until noon beneath a mountain of blankets and comforters. I was so deeply buried in my cocoon that my parents didn't always know I was still in the bed.

"Do you think she's in there?" I would hear my father say to my mother as they stood at the foot of my bed. "I mean, there is a little bit of a bump in the covers. Surely she couldn't still be asleep at this hour?" That's when I got the speech about missing the whole day. Truth be told, sleeping was a very important part of my day. My parents, for some reason, couldn't grasp this concept.

. . . . . . . . . . . . . . . . . . . . . . . . . . . . . . . . . . . . . . . .

## DEPRIVATION BEGINS

Everyone knows that newborn babies deprive you of sleep. This is a given, something you expect and try to prepare yourself for. But there's some misguided hope that this will change when the baby begins to sleep through the night. This myth is perpetuated by those who do not practice birth control. The truth is, a number of things wake children, which in turn wake adults—teething, nightmares, illness, or simply the need to have a sip of water, a pacifier, a pee, or a hug at three in the morning.

> Parents of young children wear their lack of sleep like ugly badges of courage. They are the POWs of the free, suburban world.

Parents of young children wear their lack of sleep like ugly badges of courage. They are the POWs of the free, suburban world. They are slower. Their eyes droop. They have an unlimited ability to drink coffee without getting wired. But once your child is no longer an infant, the world has little tolerance for your whiny, self-absorbed, had-just-three-hours-of-sleep self. You're expected to buck up and take it like the rest of the sorry people walking around like zombies with short fuses.

I had my children when I was thirty-three and thirty-six. I waited until I was set in my career, financially stable, wise— and very tired.

Taking into account all of the sacrifices of parenting, and there are many, I can honestly say there are very few things that I am resentful about giving up. For example, I can't just up and leave the house whenever I want to. I can't just say "screw dinner, you guys are on your own" and go have a beer in the bathtub instead. I try to take it all in stride—except for the lack of sleep. That's where I draw the line. If Mommy doesn't get enough sleep, no one is happy because Mommy turns into a bitch on wheels.

## NIGHT TERRORS

We went through a period of time when Mallory was three and having night terrors. These are nightmares where the child yells, thrashes about, and seems to be awake, but is not. Comforting children in this state is of no use because they do not register that you are there. Technically, they are still fast asleep. Oftentimes these terrors would go on for hours. Because Mallory's room was directly across from ours, there was no avoiding the racket. I would check on her periodically to make sure she was still in the bed and then go back to my bed and stare at the ceiling, listening to every outburst.

"Just make sure she's in a safe place and can't hurt herself," the doctor would say.

"But we don't have a padded room," I replied.

The night terrors soon gave way to a terror of sleeping alone. My husband and I vowed we would never have children in our bed. We know people who co-sleep with their children (a very new-age term used only by people who do it themselves). We felt that it was a situation that created dependency and an endless lack of privacy. Plus, we're too damn selfish to put up with it. I don't understand how people who sleep with their children have the opportunity to create more children. The thought of climbing over my child to have quiet sex with my husband does not appeal to me.

"Uh oh, I think she's waking up," the husband says.

"Pretend we're sleeping!" the wife says, like she's waiting for her parents to catch her screwing her high school boyfriend on the couch. Danger is fun at sixteen, not at thirty-six, at least not with your husband.

So, with the exception of illness and the occasional nightmare, we stuck to our guns about co-sleeping. We would comfort our children in their rooms and then return to our own wonderful, sacred adult bed. But Mallory's fear of going to sleep alone became so persistent we had to come up with another plan. When she was scared, we allowed her to come into our room with her sleeping bag and sleep on the floor.

The sleeping bag is a large, pink satin ballet slipper. I would be sound asleep, and suddenly, I would hear the rustle of the slick, shiny fabric being dragged across the floor, picking up stray, rough threads from the Berber carpet. She'd wedge the sleeping bag in between my side of the bed (of course) and the wall, giving me no room to get out. To go to the bathroom, I had to stealthily creep down to the end of the bed and climb over the footboard.

And then there was the teeth grinding.

*What in the world is that?* I wondered the first time I heard it.

*Gnash, gnash, gnash.* This time it was louder. I thought maybe the dog had somehow gotten into the bedroom and was gnawing on a shoe. But then I realized it was coming from Mallory. My tiny, sweet little girl with blonde ringlets.

*How could a sound like that come from a child?* I thought. It was a sound so penetrating, so annoying, it would be impossible for a sane person to sleep. It was a sound that soldiers could use to torture war criminals into giving up secrets.

"Give us your leader and we won't make you listen to this awful sound anymore," the interrogator would say, pacing around a cell, his tape recorder blaring the awful gnashing.

"Okay, okay, I'll do whatever you want, just turn it off, turn it off already!" the war criminal would scream, holding his hands over his ears.

My anxious little chip-off-the-old-block baby was grinding her teeth down to their nubs. I was officially in Hell. Because it drove me crazy almost to the point of having a nervous breakdown, I would sneak out of the room while she was in full gnash and slip into her bed (which, incidentally, is not nearly as comfortable as mine). Then she would wake up, realize I was not there, and come find me in her bed. I would wait until she fell asleep again and return to my bed. And on, and on, and on it went like that for hours.

## ON THE EDGE

Even when there are no problems with your kids sleeping through the night, you always have one ear open, listening, waiting for a problem. Mothers suffer from this. Fathers do not. A father can sleep through a baby's wail like nobody's business. I took to kicking Grif in the ankles, shouting, "Your turn!"

"Your turn, it's your turn!" I yelled. "God, don't you hear her? How can you not hear her? Are you deaf?"

Honestly, this lack-of-hearing syndrome should be no surprise. It is a genetic mutation found mostly in men. After all, they don't listen to *us*; why would they listen to a crying baby?

The problem with kicking your spouse in the ankle when the baby cries is that now you are both wide awake. He reluctantly gets up to take his turn. You lie in bed and stare at the ceiling, listening to him in the baby's room on the monitor, wondering what in the world he's doing wrong. Why in God's name is the baby still crying? I can calm her down in less than two minutes. It's not brain surgery. Rock her, rub

Honestly, this lack-of-hearing syndrome should be no surprise. It is a genetic mutation found mostly in men.

her back, and put her down. Finally, I give in and get up myself to deal with the situation. He grumpily hands Chloe to me and returns to the bedroom.

"Thanks for waking me," he grumbles as we pass in the doorway.

. . . . . . . . . . . . . . . . . . . . . . . . . . . . . . . . . . . . . . . . . . . . .

## WHITE NOISE

My newest and biggest sleep problem is Grif. I don't know if he's always been a snorer and a loud breather or if it just started to bother me when I became a hypersensitized mother with one ear always on the baby monitor. But, like Mallory's gnashing teeth, it became unbearable.

I would punch him in the shoulder and yell, "Snoring!" Usually, this made him turn over; it would stop for a moment only to start up again a few minutes later, just as I was slowly drifting back into my dream.

I tried earplugs, but they were uncomfortable and always fell out. I tried over-the-counter sleep medications, but they just made me hungover in the morning. Then we stumbled into Eden—we discovered sleep machines. Okay, maybe not quite Eden, but it's the closest thing we've found to a good night's sleep.

After two overnight sleep tests at a local lab, a doctor diagnosed Grif with sleep apnea. This means he literally stops breathing for a few moments every few seconds when he is snoring. The danger, of course, is that he might stop breathing and die. The other danger is that I might kill him first. And believe me, don't think I haven't thought about it when he's rattling away at four in the morning and I'm writing my grocery list in my head.

**The danger, of course, is that he might stop breathing and die. The other danger is that I might kill him first.**

The sleep machine has an oxygen mask that fits over your nose and mouth. It's not unlike the mask that falls down above your seat on an airplane. The mask is affixed to a big hose, which is in turn attached to the machine. In short, it forces a steady stream of air into your mouth and nose so that you can't stop breathing. This is all good except for the fact that now Grif sounds like Darth Vader. So the good news is that he's not likely to die in his sleep now, at least not from sleep apnea. The bad news is that I'm Luke Skywalker on a mission to eradicate the evil force from my bed.

My miracle solution jumped right out in front of me one day in an unlikely place—the mall. I was browsing in Brookstone with my mother. The salesman showed us a fancy noise machine with babbling brooks, thunderstorms, chirping crickets, and more. My mother knew about my sleep issues and insisted on buying one for both of us.

"Have you tried the 'serenity' setting?" she said. "It's just like being at the spa. It's *sooooooo* relaxing."

"No, Mother, white noise, that's what I like," I told her for the one-hundredth time. "That's the only thing that blocks everything else. I told you I didn't need the fancy machine, just a humidifier on high without water!"

She spent nearly $100 on the machine, so I can understand why she might be disappointed that I'm not open to trying the other sounds. But it's just not going to happen. When I listen to ocean or rain, my brain focuses on the pattern and I can't sleep. I need mindless noise that blocks everything, I mean absolutely everything, out.

The bad, or good, side effect of the wind tunnel, as we now affectionately refer to our bedroom, is that we can't hear Mallory and Chloe. If Mallory needs us, she can just run across the hall and tap one of us (most likely me) on the shoulder. But not hearing Chloe, the baby, is not an option. To override the machine sounds, we put the baby monitor on high. This means when she does cry it sounds like a wild animal being bludgeoned to death in the jungle. It's not a pretty thing to wake up to. But it gets your attention.

. . . . . . . . . . . . .

If we're being really candid, I think most of us would agree that sleeping alone is the best way to get solid rest. Because then it's all about you, not about what the other person is doing that might disrupt you. But as long as I'm a wife and a mother, I think the nights of sleeping alone will be few and far between.

Don't think I don't take advantage of business trips. I crank the air in the hotel room, move to the center of the bed like a queen on her throne, and lie spread-eagle across the mattress, just because I can.

nother Day, Another
Poop Missile

*"The way I see it, if you want the rainbow,
you gotta put up with the rain."*
—Dolly Parton

"How was your day?" I asked Grif, stabbing a meatball with my fork.

"Good, busy, fine. How about yours?" he asked as he drenched his salad with low-fat dressing.

"Same, busy. This morning was crazy though: Chloe pooped in her pants right as I was walking out the door." I dipped my bread into a pool of marinara sauce on the plate. "It was everywhere, down her legs, soaked into her socks, even in her sneakers. I had to hold her away from me so I wouldn't get it on my suit."

"Gross," he said, "really, really gross."

Before you have children you have very few conversations about poop. It's just not something people generally like to talk about. But once you bring a child into the world, all bodily functions are fair game. It's hard to ignore something that you're elbow deep in the majority of the time.

"How was your night?" my neighbor asks as she steadies the handlebars on her son's bike.

"Pretty good," I reply, "except Chloe's got that thing going around, you know, diarrhea every few hours." I tighten the strap of Mallory's bike helmet beneath her chin, inadvertently pinching her skin.

"Ow, Mommy!" she screams. "That hurts!"

"Yeah, our kids had that too, real runny, kind of green, nasty," my neighbor says as she watches her son ride full throttle into a ditch. "It's going around."

. . . . . . . . . . . . . . . . . . . . . . . . . . . . . . . . . . . . . . . . . . .

## POTTY WORSHIP

From diapers to potty training, parents of young children become obsessed with going to the bathroom. Sometimes I think about how many diapers I have changed. Thousands, I would guess. And it's not something you get credit for. Your kids don't grow up and say, "Gee Mom, thanks for wiping my ass all those years, I really appreciate it."

And it's not just changing the diapers—it's the leaky diapers, the accidents in the underwear, the soaked clothes, the wet sheets. Basically we spend most of our children's young lives inventing ways to keep the poop contained.

We thought our first daughter, Mallory, was a genius when she peed in her potty at eighteen months. Of course she wasn't really potty trained for another year and a half. So we spent countless hours sitting with her in the bathroom, pleading with her to go on demand—apparently a very hard concept to grasp.

It doesn't seem all that hard to me. If I haven't peed in the last five minutes, I'm pretty much open to it anytime. Not the case with young kids. You can make pee sounds with your mouth, turn on the faucet to simulate the sound of pee, or give them copious amounts of water to drink. It doesn't work.

We kept thinking Mallory was trained. Like taking training wheels off a bike too early, we put her in underwear way before she was steady enough to make it through a day without backup. This mistake was followed by weeks of changing her clothes several times a day and changing the sheets every other day.

> Basically we spend most of our children's young lives inventing ways to keep the poop contained.

To curb the nighttime pee problem we put Mallory in Pull-Ups, you know, the diapers shaped like underwear. If this isn't the biggest gimmick on the market, I don't know what is. The goal is for kids to treat Pull-Ups like underwear, but instead Pull-Ups give kids leeway to have accidents, to pee in an expensive diaper, over and over again. Why would a child get out of a warm, comfortable bed to pee when she could pee in her pants and not wet the bed?

During Mallory's potty training period, we carried a portable potty in the car. I was as big a fan of this object as I was of the minivan. I felt like it was giving up the last vestige I had of my cool self. It's hard to be cool alongside a busy road standing next to a two-year-old on a miniature potty. But like most other things parents do after saying they will never do it, the portable potty chair was part of crisis management.

"I have to go," Mallory screams from the backseat.

"Can't you wait until we eat lunch?" Grif replies, running his fingers through already-manic hair. "Just ten more minutes, Sweetie, hang in there."

With the precision of a NASCAR pit crew, we work together to keep the kid and the car seat dry.

"No," she screams, kicking the back of the seat with her light-up sneakers. "I have to go now!"

"Stop the car," I say, grabbing the dashboard. "All of the extra clothes are in the luggage wedged under the stroller. I can't get to them. She's got nothing else to wear!"

"Fine!" he says, screeching to the muddy side of the road. "You get her, I'll get the potty."

With the precision of a NASCAR pit crew, we work together to keep the kid and the car seat dry. Grif grabs the seat and the toilet. I grab Mallory and the Barbie. Within seconds we are set up and ready for the main event.

"Too late, Mommy," Mallory says, pointing to the big wet spot on the back of her pants, "I already went."

## THE FINAL FRONTIER

Mallory eventually mastered peeing in the potty with just a few slips here and there. But pooping was another thing entirely.

We finally realized she was *afraid* to poop in the potty. So instead, she would hold it and then go in the Pull-Up when she really needed to go. This meant every morning I had to bend down with my big pregnant belly and wipe adult-size poop out of her butt.

"Do you know how hard this is for Mommy?" I would say, grimacing and steadying myself with one hand on the side of the tub.

"It's yucky, Mommy," she would say, holding her own nose with one hand and waving away the smell with the other. "Get it away from me."

Clearly, she didn't get that there was a way out of the predicament for both of us. But for some reason she had a mental and emotional roadblock to our shared sanity.

So I did what all mothers do when they are in a quandary. I sought knowledge.

"How's the pooping in the potty thing going with Miranda?" I said to my girlfriend at the office.

"No problems, she knows when she has to go. No accidents at all," she says, confidently flipping her long blonde hair over one shoulder with a quick turn of her head. Like a game-show hostess.

"Did you have any stumbling blocks getting to that point? Any fear or trepidation?"

I nervously pull loose strands of hair back into a my messy ponytail.

"Not really, nope, not that I can think of," she says, her hands squarely on her tiny hips.

She was, and is, a good friend, but at this moment I wanted to wash that calm smile off her perfect little face. Hell hath no fury like a woman with raging hormones and a three-year-old who is still pooping in her pants.

I even signed up for a seminar at my pediatrician's office about how to get your kid to poop in the potty. The doctor told me to try giving her a laxative to keep her from holding it in all day. To me, this sounded like more poop for me to clean up, not more success on the porcelain throne. I read books, scoured the Internet, and tried to reason with her. One book said that girls have a hard time pooping on the potty because they feel like they are losing part of themselves, part of their bodies. Honestly, it's not a part I want to keep.

We bought a video from Duke University about going to the bathroom. Researchers actually put this thing together to help parents with these sticky situations. It is full of 1980s families with feathered hair and dated clothes singing songs like "I'm a Super-Duper Pooper" and "On Top of My Potty." Although *I* found it a little disturbing, it seemed to give Mallory the tools and confidence to push to the other side. We even had a cassette tape that we played in the car. I found myself humming "Super-Duper Pooper" on my way to work well after I had left the day care.

Grif hated cleaning up more than I did. So, one week while I was on a business trip, he refused to allow Mallory to wear Pull-Ups. As a result, she was forced to poop in the potty. This actually worked! Grif considered himself a genius after this accomplishment. I had to agree.

Even now, if I don't remind Mallory to use the bathroom before she goes to sleep, she wets the bed.

"Mommy, you may need to change my sheets," she'll say. "I sweated a lot last night."

"Sweetie, it's pee," I say without judgment as I touch the pumpkin-size spot in the middle of the bed.

"No, it's sweat," she retorts, trying to smooth down her wild cowlick at her hairline with her palm and some spit.

"Whatever," I say as I strip the soiled sheets.

## COMING AROUND AGAIN

Here's the real rub—I'm facing it again with Chloe. It seems like potty training should be something you only have to do once in your lifetime. There should be a decree from God: "She did it once, and from here on out all her children will be miraculously potty trained at birth!"

We started later this time, around age two.

In the beginning she was very hard on herself. "Try potty!" she yelled when she got up in the morning. "C'mon, pee-pee," she said, pushing in on her stomach with both hands as she sat.

For the first few months she went on the toilet only twice. We were pretty sure it was by accident both times. But we still cheered and did the pee-pee dance anyway to reinforce the accomplishment. Not unlike watching Mallory pee in a portable potty on the side of the road, doing the pee-pee dance dashes any thoughts you ever had of being cool again.

Then we got slack. Call it the second-child syndrome, call it wanting her to be a baby forever, but the reality is that we just got too damn busy to keep working at it.

"I want to go potty," Chloe would say.

"No, Mommy's too busy, why don't you just pee in your diaper," I said, thinking it's much easier than finding a bathroom in Wal-Mart.

But now we're back in the saddle. She actually woke up one day and announced she wanted to wear some of the pretty Dora the Explorer underwear I had bought for her at Wal-Mart. I think her exact words were: "I want to cover my butt with Dora!"

I took Chloe to day care and explained our new predicament to the teachers. Like troopers in the trenches of war, they told me to bring it on, just bring a lot of extra underwear and pants to school.

"We get paid to wipe up poop," said Miss Adele. "That's part of our job. But if it's real runny, do you want me to wash out the underwear or just throw it away?"

I told her to definitely throw it away. And I made a mental note to buy cheaper underwear.

Now, when Chloe comes home from school in mismatched outfits—stripes and flowers, let's say—I immediately know there's been an accident. When I ask her about it, she enthusiastically tells me she went to the bathroom in her pants and had to be changed. I know how this happens. I've seen her do it at home. All of a sudden she looks down with wide eyes at the urine pooling at her feet, like she simply can't imagine where it's coming from. My recently refinished hardwood floors are taking a beating.

Others have caught on, too. When we visited my mother's house in Philadelphia with her pristine cream-colored shag carpets, and I told her Chloe was in underwear, she suggested we put her in a garbage bag, tie it around her waist, and cut holes for the feet. I'm not kidding. She honestly said this.

"Can't you just put her in a Pull-Up while she's here?" my mom said, tilting her head for emphasis. "Or we could put newspaper down."

"Mom," I said, "she's not a *dog*." I said, trying to figure out if she was serious. "Plus, I don't want her to backslide."

She didn't have far to slide. Within a couple of hours, Chloe had pooped and peed on my mother's carpet, ottoman, and couch. Soon my mother was at the drugstore, asking the cashier what product she could buy to get human pee stains out of her carpet and upholstery.

. . . . . . . . . . . . . . . . . . . . . . . . . . . . . . . . . . . . . . .

## POOP MISSILE

Chloe has also become fond of pooping in the tub. This is a horror that's almost impossible to describe until you've experienced it yourself.

"Poop in the tub, poop in the tub," she screams, as if a submarine has mysteriously invaded her bubble bath.

I come running, my eyes darting through the holes in the bubbles. It's there, it's gone, it's there. I quickly scoop Chloe out of the contaminated water and wrap her in a towel. Again, I scan the water for the poop missile that I know will disintegrate in minutes if I don't remove it. I grab a wad of paper towels and reach in, parting the bubbles with my other hand.

*Another day, another child rescued from a poop missile.*

"Get it, Mommy, hurry, get it," a dripping Chloe yells from her perch on the footstool. Clearly, she still has no connection to this poop that submerged itself in her formerly clean, soapy water.

Finally, I grab it with the wad of now soaked paper towels. I wince at the thought of what I am touching and toss it into the nearby toilet.

"Good job, Mommy, good job," Chloe yells, clapping her tiny hands beneath the towel.

It's just another day for a mother. Another day, another child rescued from a poop missile.

. . . . . . . . . . . . . . . . . . . . . . . . . . . . . . . . . . . . . . . . . . . .

## THE LIGHT . . . WELL, ALMOST

Chloe is almost completely potty trained now. Our last hurdle is getting her through the night dry. She's averaging about two nights of dryness for every one night of wetting the bed—two steps forward, one step back. Though the odds aren't so good, I'm simply done with diapers or Pull-Ups of any kind. I'm seeing the light at the end of this potty training tunnel.

As a stopgap measure, I purchased waterproof pads that are about the size of a welcome mat. You place them right on top of the fitted sheet so that if the child pees, you don't have to change the sheets. But here's the catch: You still have to change the child.

"Mommy, I'm weeeeeeeeeeeeet!" Chloe screams at the side of my bed. She's about three inches from my face. Past her, the clock on the nightstand reads 3:30 a.m.

"Okay, okay, I'm coming," I say, stumbling out of bed. I pull her nightgown over her head with one hand and her wet underwear down with the other hand. In the dark I stumble into her room, find wipes, clean underwear, and a T-shirt. When the process is over, she does not want to return to her bed, so against my better judgment I bring her into our bed. Of course, we have no waterproof pad on our bed.

"What's that?" Grif says and rolls over. He lifts his wet hand up into the air as if he's been poisoned. When he sees Chloe curled up against my back, he immediately knows the answer.

## THREE'S A CROWD

When you have small kids, you have no privacy in the bathroom. It is not uncommon for both of my girls to sit at my feet when I'm on the toilet. When they were babies, I held them as I went. Now we have conversations about their day, what they want for dinner, and what books they want to read that evening. Asking them to leave is a joke. They assume that because I sit with them while they go, they should return the favor. I draw the line, however, at bringing in friends.

"Privacy!" I yell as I hear Mallory and her friend about to storm into my bathroom.

"Why?" she asks, no matter how many times we've had the same conversation.

"Because I said so," I say, trying to finish my business before the invasion.

The lack of privacy in the bathroom was a big deal for me to get over. I don't even like my *husband* to be in the bathroom when I go. I can barely stand public restrooms. Now I have company there, too. Mallory and Chloe want to know why Mommy crouches above public toilet seats instead of sitting down.

"When can I stand and pee?" Mallory asks.

"When you're tall enough," I say. "Plus, you have to have strong quads."

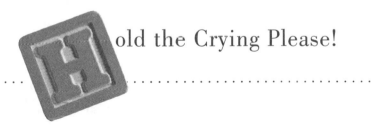

# old the Crying Please!

*"Never face facts, if you do you'll never
get up in the morning."*
—Marlo Thomas

Leaving the house with a baby or child could be compared to flying a plane on acid. Both are completely unpredictable and unadvisable situations.

First, the preparation to leave the house is so daunting it's almost not worth the effort. If you have a baby, you pack diapers, pacifiers, bottles, extra clothes. For a toddler you need snacks, drinks, and an endless supply of toys or books to keep them happy while you attempt to do your errands. And don't forget the gear—strollers, car seats, portable high chairs. Whether you're leaving for fifteen minutes or three days, the preparation is pretty much the same. In fact, the preparation can sometimes take more time than the actual errands, leaving you annoyed, frustrated, and sorry you ever left the house.

Here's an idea: Stay home for the first five years, except when you have your husband or babysitter home with the child. There's no need to expose the world to children before they're ready to exist without imposing themselves upon others. There's no need for me to have all that anxiety about trying to make them behave in public. I wonder if companies would consider a five-year maternity leave.

"Honey," I say to my husband, "let's just wait until they're at least five. When they're older, we can go anywhere we want, do anything. For now I say we just stay home. We can shop on the Internet, order movies, get takeout. What do you say?" He just smiles a tired smile and shakes his head like it's the first good idea I've had in a long time.

But eventually you do it. You leave the compound, knowing it could be a disaster. After Mallory was born, I thought taking her out as a baby was the hardest thing I would ever do. She weighed about seven pounds, but the carrier weighed about twenty. I don't weigh very much myself, so schlepping the carrier around on my bony arm left me with a bad case of bulging discs. Hauling it up into the backseat of the SUV was almost more than I could handle. What I really needed was a small forklift to get the thing into the car, but I settled for swinging the carrier in one fierce motion up into the seat, hoping neither of us would get whiplash.

*How do I return the grocery cart when my baby is in the car and I am afraid to leave her?*

In the beginning I struggled with questions like: *How do I return the grocery cart when my baby is in the car and I am afraid to leave her?* Answer: You don't. Wedge it in between the parking spaces and pray it doesn't roll into someone else's car; at least make sure if it does, no one sees you. *What do you do if the baby starts to scream and you've got a full cart of groceries?* Answer: Let her scream. You're not coming back to shop from scratch. *Getting ugly stares?* Answer: Ignore them, because they were crying babies once, too. Since most babies are about the size of a football when they are balled up, putting the kid on your shoulder usually works wonders. By the time Chloe came along, I had perfected this to where I could balance her on my shoulder like an accessory, scan my debit card, and talk on the cell phone.

Really, in the beginning, a baby has about as much personality as a Target purse—just cute in a functional kind of way. The last thing you want to do is attract attention to it. Low profile, that's what you're going for. Take it out only when absolutely necessary.

## PUBLIC NUISANCE

Even for someone who has children, a crying child in public is about as annoying as it gets. It's like flies buzzing around your salad at an outdoor restaurant or a high-pitched alarm clock waking you up when you've got a hangover. This is especially true when it's someone else's child.

I learned my lesson on this one the hard way and picked a battle that I eventually lost. My friend and I visited a children's museum one Friday morning and afterward decided to get a bite to eat at a small, casual restaurant across the street. It was 11:00 a.m., a time when no normal adult would be eating lunch. As we walked in, Mallory, who was eighteen months old at the time, began to have a temper tantrum. Luckily, we were the only ones in the restaurant, so I went ahead and ordered, hopeful that she would calm down when I offered her pretzels.

While we were waiting for our food, Mallory continued to rant and rave on the floor next to us. Either because I had become numb to her frequent outbursts, or I was just too damn tired, I did nothing. I slowly sipped my lemonade and chatted with my girlfriend, hoping the storm would pass.

After a couple minutes, the owner of the restaurant came out and told me she just couldn't take it anymore, that I would have to leave. She stood there with her hands on her hips, glaring at Mallory. I was shocked. I looked around the restaurant: not a soul in sight, except for a stoned-looking group of hippies in bandannas making our havarti on sunflower-seed bread sandwiches. What happened to "the customer is always right" or "the customer comes first"? More stunned than indignant, I left.

But the story doesn't end there. It should have. But like a dog with a fresh bone, I simply couldn't let it go. After reflecting upon the incident—yes, stewing—I decided to make a complaint with the Better Business Bureau, just to give the woman a little grief for what I considered to be an unprofessional attitude on her part. Big mistake.

My reasoning was actually well-founded; my understanding of the potential fallout was not. Clearly, anyone has the right to refuse service in their private business, but it's not smart business to throw people out of your restaurant unless they are presenting a problem for *other* customers. That was not the case in this situation.

Had the restaurant owner said, "I can see you're having a rough morning, would you like me to pack that lunch for you to go?" I would have gotten the hint and taken it without such offense. Sure, I might have still been a little miffed, but I would have gotten over it pretty quickly.

Turns out, I should have let it go. A mutual friend heard my story and passed it along to a local newspaper columnist. She contacted me and wanted to do an interview with me about the incident. With vengeance in my heart and no common sense in my head, I agreed. But I told her I could not use my television name (my maiden name) because I had to separate the issue from my job. I was speaking to her not as a television reporter but as a mother.

Predictably, the whole thing backfired. Not only did she get loads of angry mail supporting the restaurant owner, but she also wrote a follow-up column berating me for disrupting a public place with a little she-devil who is obviously in need of some serious parenting. The topic even became fodder for local radio morning shows. It was pretty awful.

When I didn't think it could get any worse, a local independent newspaper figured out the connection between the mother in the column and my identity as a television reporter. He wrote a column saying that two members of the media, the editorial writer and I, had conspired to unfairly bring this hardworking business owner down and had been deceptive about my identity in the process. My managers were not amused.

Like everything else, it eventually went away. People found something else to talk about. Needless to say, I will not be visiting *that* soapbox again, and I sure do miss havarti on sunflower-seed bread.

. . . . . . . . . . . . . . . . . . . . . . . . . . . . . . . . . . . . . . . . . . . . . . .

## MELTING DOWN

The truth is when you leave the house with children, you never really know what's going to happen. You can be the most organized, most prepared mother on the face of the earth and still not anticipate the out-of-this-world needs that will inevitably come up.

"I need a ball," two-year-old Chloe yells from the backseat. "Ball, ball, ball!" her voice rises to a fever pitch. I turn up the radio and try to think about where I might get a frigging ball.

Screw cell phones and drunk drivers: The most dangerous person behind the wheel of a car is a mother with her kids in the car.

"Mommy, did you bring those puffy, sparkly star stickers? I need one," five-year-old Mallory whines from the backseat. "And I'm dying of thirst, for real, seriously dying. I need a drink now!"

*So do I, honey,* I say to myself. *Light on the ice, heavy on the liquor.*

This usually happens when I'm going about sixty-five in the left lane of a highway with bumper-to-bumper traffic all around me. Screw cell phones and drunk drivers: The most dangerous person behind the wheel of a car is a mother with her kids in the car. There's no distraction that can even match it. On a good day, I'm tossing fries at them and reaching behind my seat to find a crayon that's dropped on the floor. On an average day I just crank up the tunes and tune it out.

"I ain't saying she's a gold digger," the radio blares.

"Red crayon!" Chloe yells.

"But I ain't seen her with no broke—"

"She hit me and I need juice or I'm going to die!" Mallory yells.

My rearview mirror is on my kids, not on the traffic. I also have a huge blind spot from the sunshade on Chloe's window because she is supersensitive to light. Occasionally, a shoe or sock flies over the headrest, followed by a piercing scream— "Shoe, shoe, shoe!"

## ON THE WRONG SIDE OF THE LAW

One afternoon when Mallory was a baby, I was rushing home for naptime after trying to squeeze one too many errands into a small window of time. Mallory was screaming like she was being poked with small needles all over her body. In my mad dash to get home, I inadvertently breezed through a stop sign in my neighborhood. A cop pulled me over. On cue, the second the car stopped, Mallory stopped crying. She was trying to make me look bad. Terrorists train young.

"Officer," I said, wearily tucking back the hair that had fallen out of my messy ponytail. "My daughter is exhausted, I'm just trying to get her home for a nap. And besides that she has a poop!" As soon as I said it, I thought maybe I should have held that part back. Screw it, holding back is not one of my strong suits.

He stood with his hands on his thick hips, sizing me up behind his oversized mirrored sunglasses.

"License and registration please," he said. He was going to have none of my privileged-white-suburban-hysterical-mother act. I sense that I'm actually going to get a ticket and there is nothing I can do about it.

I hand him what he asks for without another word, and in the rearview mirror I watch him return to his cruiser. Then I decide to take some action. I get Mallory out of the car seat, open up the back of the Ford Explorer, and proceed to change her huge poop in full view of the patrol car. I take my time, laying out the changing mat, the wipes, and a bag to dispose of the diaper. I wipe my brow several times with the back of my hand to give him the full impact of what it is like to change a diaper in the back of a car. I suspect he's never done it.

In short, I make it look hard, really hard. I make it look like this diaper might be the thing to send me over the edge, the thing that made me blow the stop sign. After all, I wasn't in my right mind; I had a screaming child with a stinky diaper in the backseat, who could blame me? I'll tell you who, Boss Hog, that's who.

He takes a long time to return to my car, and with good reason. He is probably afraid to be near the poopy diaper and equally as afraid to be near the stressed-out mother. When he finally does return, he sheepishly hands me a warning. I won. Guess he realized my life was stinky enough without getting a ticket.

I had another brush with the law several years later when Mallory was four and a half. This time I got confused about the lanes at a stoplight in a little yuppie beach town called Stone Harbor. To make matters worse, I had brought my beach bag and had forgotten my wallet and license. It was a holiday and the cop had to "run" my license in the computer.

Unfortunately, Mallory was not yet old enough to read the nuances of the situation. When the cop called for backup, she went ballistic and started screaming at the top of her lungs.

"Don't take my mommy to jail!" she wailed over and over. It's no wonder that she thought I was going to jail. For years I've been using the law to bully her into doing things she didn't want to do. *If you don't ride in the car seat, Mommy will go to jail. If you don't wear a coat on a cold day, Mommy will go to jail. If you don't eat your peas, Mommy will go to jail.* It's more likely that Mommy would get a visit from social services, but that's harder to explain.

On this particular day it was obvious to the cop that I was a threat, possibly a terrorist threat cleverly disguised in a cute beach hat. Something had to be done about me and my terrorist child. After all, what a clever disguise—a Volvo, a cute hat, and a cute (albeit wailing) kid. Who would suspect us? But Mr. Summer-Rent-a-Cop was clearly not born yesterday. He was on my case and nothing was going to slip by his gut instincts.

"Don't take my mommy to jail!" Mallory screamed again, pointing her finger at the officer through the open window. Her face was red and puffy. Tears rolled down her cheeks. "You'll be sorry!" she added for emphasis, punching the air.

I tried to negotiate with the cop. I offered to let him follow me to my father's house to get my license. I explained that my husband was at home with a sleeping baby and could not bring it to me.

The cop was flustered by Mallory's outbursts every time he got close to the car. He would approach and then step back abruptly as if he were being shocked by an invisible fence. Maybe he just couldn't take Mallory's screaming anymore. Maybe he finally decided I was not a suicide bomber. For whatever reason, he let me go. He agreed not to give me a ticket for running the red light, just for not having my license. At the time this sounded like a good deal. After all, I had broken the law. I assumed the ticket would be about $25. As I pulled away I glanced at the cost—$175! It was an expensive lesson. Always carry your license in Stone Harbor.

To this day Mallory is terrified of police officers. She is worried that I will be arrested and she will be left to fend for herself. Luckily, I think she is smart enough to find her way home. On the plus side, she's always pointing out speed traps wherever we go.

"There's one, Mommy, a cop, right there under the bridge, you better slow down," she yells, with growing anxiety in her voice.

She's better than a radar detector.

## AND THE BEAT GOES ON

Leaving the house with one child seems like nothing once you have multiple children. My learning curve after Chloe was much faster. It had to be, by necessity. Mallory had places to go, and I wasn't going to let a baby get in the way.

At first, I braved the two-child thing in public like a hero. I'd strap the baby in my front carrier, hold Mallory's hand, and head out to just about anywhere with a fully stocked diaper bag. But things changed as Chloe approached two. Just when I was confident that Mallory would stay by my side in public, not act up, and occasionally help me, Chloe had her own agenda.

When I think about it, it's not really one or the other child who is the problem. They both have their moments. But one-on-one they're both pretty good kids. It's the combination that sends me to the edge of the cliff. It's the tandem screaming, the tandem whining, and the tandem fighting.

People are always asking, how do your girls get along? Are they best friends? I don't tell them about the near-death experiences that Chloe has experienced at Mallory's hands. I don't tell them how Chloe is always taunting her older sister in a singsong voice learned from her friends at preschool. I don't tell them how it's rare for more than ten minutes to go by without one tattling on the other. Instead I say: They love each other! Just like a drug addict in denial, I hope that by the end of my twelve-step life, if I say it enough it will be true.

In the end we can't control our kids; we can only control how we react to them. And because we're human beings, we are not always going to react well. I threaten them with spankings, sending them to their rooms, taking something away . . . but once the crying starts it's almost impossible to stop.

Today, however, I found something that worked. I officially lost my mind and it felt good. Mallory was whining in the backseat that she didn't want to help Chloe open her juice box, that it wasn't her job. As she continued to whine, two balloons we'd bought at the grocery store kept bopping me in the head and obstructing my peripheral vision. I told the girls to keep the frigging balloons out of the front seat because they were distracting me from watching the road. As Mallory's whining reached a fever pitch, I did what every mother who has officially lost it thinks about doing: I opened the sunroof and released the girls' balloons, watching them spiral upward toward the clouds.

> I opened the sunroof and released the girls' balloons, watching them spiral upward toward the clouds.

"Noooooooooooooooooo!" Mallory wailed from the backseat.

I smiled and turned up the radio. It felt good.

# o Guilt, No Glory

*"Reality is something you rise above."*
—Liza Minnelli

All my life people have been telling me to let go of guilt, that it's not healthy. But I disagree. Guilt, not unlike pain, is an essential component of what drives us often to do the right thing, the thing we may not want to do but need to do. So I embrace guilt for all that it is and all that it has given me. Plus, I'm a world-class martyr, a title I've worn proudly for most of my life.

Guilt is an integral part of parenting, especially for working mothers. It must be recognized and dealt with accordingly.

Mallory gave me a verbal list of reasons why I should not work. First on the list: She could be on the swim team at the neighborhood pool. My six-year-old saw her need to dog-paddle from one side of the pool to the other with seventy-five kids as more important than my career.

"But, Mommy, they get numbers painted on their arms," she says in a pleading tone.

> Guilt is an integral part of parenting, especially for working mothers.

The practices and the meets are at times that I cannot make because of my work schedule. I've thought about trying to work it out some other way, believe me, I have. But the hoops I would have to jump through to make it happen are insane and would *still* make me late for work. Plus, I don't think she has Olympic swimmer potential, so denying this early exposure to the sport is not derailing her intended career.

"Harry is on the swim team, Mommy," she says, hands perched on little hips.

"I know, sweetie. Harry's mom doesn't work."

"Billy is on the swim team."

"His mother works out of the house and has more flexibility than I do," I say, repeating information that she has already heard a dozen times.

"Well, I think you need to leave early or quit your job so I can be on the swim team," she says with a serious look on her face.

"Mommy is on the news, honey. It's on at six every night. I can't just leave to take you to swim team," I say, not even convincing myself that what I do is that important.

"Can't *somebody else* do the news?" she asks, looking me directly in the eye.

The other items on Mallory's list of why I need to quit my job include not having to rush in the morning, not having to go to a before-and-after-school program, and, most importantly, the fact that I would be available to have lunch with her every day in the elementary school cafeteria.

"Honey, you know I wouldn't come every day," I say, imagining soggy chicken nuggets, runny mashed potatoes, and screaming kids, not to mention the cafeteria smell that hasn't changed since I was in elementary school.

"Why not, what else would you have to do?" She throws her hands open wide to the ceiling.

"I'd have lots of stuff to do," I say. "Take care of the house, take care of Chloe."

"Wait, you mean *she* would be home with you?" Mallory says, a tinge of jealousy and anger in her voice.

"Sure," I say. "I mean, I'm not going to pay for day care if I'm not working. That wouldn't make any sense."

"Well, if Chloe was home you wouldn't do anything fun with her without me, would you?" she asks with growing agitation in her voice. "Like go to the pool or the park?"

"What do you want us to do, sit home and do nothing?" I say, putting my hand on her shoulder. "I can't promise that we wouldn't do anything fun, I mean, that's just crazy, honey."

"Okay then, I definitely want you to keep working, forget swim team," she says, resolute in her decision. Clearly, the girl has her priorities.

. . . . . . . . . . . . . . . . . . . . . . . . . . . . . . . . . . . . . . . . .

## MY REASONS

My reasons for wanting to work are not as inspired as Mallory's list for not wanting me to, but they are important to me. I explained to Mallory that a big part of me is what I do for a living, that it helps define me and makes me who I am. Without it I might be a person she might not like and, more importantly, a person I might not like—you know, an alcoholic, *Jerry Springer*–watching, depressed person.

This is not an easy concept for a six-year-old to understand. Honestly, it's not an easy concept for a forty-year-old, but it's the closest that I've come to understanding why the struggle is worth it. I just know when I'm at the park and see mothers happily playing with their children, feeding them Goldfish, wiping runny noses, and tying little sneakers, I think, *Thank God this isn't my life every day.* It's a fun place to visit on my day off. But I couldn't live in it day in, day out. I admire the mothers who can do it and do it well; I'm just not one of them. I'm sure their kids won't need therapy nearly as early as mine.

In short, what I get from work makes me a better mother, and what I get from being a mother makes me a better journalist. At least that's my story and I'm sticking to it. So bring on the heavy guilt—I've got a strong back.

## LEARNING TO RUSH

One thing from Mallory's list that is right on target is the fact that being a working mother means my children are always in a perpetual state of rushing. Once I get my caffeine buzz going in the morning, I rev my engine and switch into high gear. Just the sight of Chloe lying on the couch in her nightgown lazily watching cartoons is enough to send me over the edge. I run back to Mallory's bedroom where she lies cocooned in her comforter. That's when the screaming starts. It's like someone has flipped a switch and I become frenetic.

I rush them through breakfast, constantly asking if they're finished eating.

"Are you done with your waffle, Chloe?" I ask, with the plate poised over the garbage can.

"Noooooooooo," she screams, lunging for the soggy, half-eaten waffle.

I rush them through dressing, pulling shirts over little heads, helping to button, tie, and zip. Throughout the process

I'm bombarded with arguments about not wanting to wear pants, not liking a certain shirt, and not wanting to wear a coat.

"I want to wear shorts," Chloe screeches, refusing to put her legs in the pants of her jeans.

"It's fifty degrees, you can't wear shorts," I say. "Mommy will go to jail if I send you to school in shorts." This is my standard answer for all things that cannot be explained quickly or easily to their satisfaction. Jail they get. It works.

Brushing teeth and brushing hair prompts another skirmish, but I'm armed and ready. "Your teeth will fall out if you don't brush," I say with conviction. "It's time to go."

"We *know*, Mommy," Mallory says as she casually runs a brush through her knotted hair. As much as I hate that expression about hair looking like a bird's nest, Mallory's truly does when she wakes up. I can't figure out who she is wrestling with in the middle of the night to get so many knots.

"So if you know, why are you moving so slowly?" I say as I pull Chloe's nightgown over her head. She is transfixed by Clifford and doesn't react except for the moment the garment shields her eyes from the screen.

"Clifford!" she screams, her voice muffled. I quickly pull a shirt over her head and she returns to her television-watching trance.

"I'm moving as fast as I can," Mallory says as she leans back into the cushions on the couch and puts the hairbrush in her lap. "Why do we always have to rush anyway?"

"Because, as I've told you four hundred times, Mommy works. I can't be late for work; I have to be in court at 9:00 a.m." Once again, I'm stunned by my need to justify myself to a six-year-old. "Stop messing around and get dressed, make your bed, and brush your teeth!"

"I can't do *all* that," she whines.

"Sure you can," I say, carrying the breakfast dishes from the table to the sink. This is something that they are supposed to do, but like many other things I expect them to do, they won't do it fast enough, so I just do it myself. It's just one more notch on my martyrdom belt.

I'll pull up next to a trucker. I think he's smiling at me and then realize he's laughing about all the crap in my car.

"You're mean, Mommy," Mallory says, stomping off in the direction of her bedroom.

"I know, I know," I say to no one in particular.

We race to the car with book bags, coats, lunches, and Chloe's stuffed animals. Chloe never leaves the house without at least one or two items from her room. The way I look at it, it's her version of a purse and cell phone, and not worth fighting about. The stuff ends up piling up in my car throughout the week—rubber ducks, stuffed dogs, and plastic people. I'll pull up next to a trucker. I think he's smiling at me and then realize he's laughing about all the crap in my car. Once again I hear that mantra in my head: *I am not cool anymore.*

"Hurry, girls, hurry, get into the car," I say. "Mommy's got to go to work!"

I push their little butts up into their car seats and frantically buckle them in. I understand how important it is for children to be safe in the car, but I don't understand why they make the seat belts so complicated that you have to have an engineering degree to buckle them.

This frantic race to the car is usually followed by one or two more trips back into the house to grab something I forgot—my Blackberry, Mallory's homework, Chloe's brown sock for a class project. By the time they get to school and I get to work, we're all exhausted from so much rushing. In these moments it's hard to believe it's all worth it. It makes me feel a little guilty pushing them so hard. But then I push that guilt aside and go on with my day. What choice do I have?

## HURRY UP AND RELAX

The evenings and weekends are not much better when it comes to rushing. It's as if I can't turn it off; there's just so much stuff swirling around my brain that I need to do, and there's never enough time to do it.

In the evening I get home late and am usually greeted by a messy house and children who are hungry and need baths. I've got to put it into high gear. I have to psych myself up before I walk in the door because I know as soon as I do that I'm on deck. That's the price I pay for working. When I'm home, I'm steering the ship, fearing if I don't, we're liable to hit an iceberg. Plus, the guilt of not being with the kids all day drives me to overachieve.

"Come on, girls, eat your fish sticks so we can take a bath," I say as Chloe dances around the kitchen, waving a fish stick in the air like a wand. My blood sugar is plummeting. I haven't yet eaten myself. I think I had a salad with chicken around 11:30 that morning, but I can't really remember.

"Don't like sticks, Mommy," Chloe smiles.

"I'm not hungry," Mallory says, pushing her chair back from the table.

I've had it. I don't care. "Eat it or go hungry," I say. "There are children starving somewhere in the world. We'll send it to them." God, I'm really turning into my mother.

Come on over, read to my children. I dare you. At my house it's a raucous fight about how many books, what books, and who gets to pick them.

After dinner, there's bath time, which for the girls is more about getting Mommy's attention than about getting clean. There's lots of splashing and screaming. There's water on the floor and soap in someone's eyes. And then there's the fight about getting out. Once they are in the tub, they never want to get out because that makes bedtime closer.

After the bath, there's usually a lot of crying and whining associated with combing wet, tangled hair. I threaten to cut their hair short if they can't handle a little pain. Again, I'm turning into my mother. But unlike my daughters, I *wanted* a short pageboy haircut (rather than the Farrah Fawcett feathered look that was in at the time).

After bath, hair-combing, tooth-brushing, and pajamas, it's reading time. This is supposed to be a quiet, special bonding time, as advertised in public service announcements where a child is happily perched on a parent's lap near the caption "Read to Your Child." Come on over, read to my children. I dare you. At my house it's a raucous fight about how many books, what books, and who gets to pick them. Once these battles have been fought and a truce is negotiated, I am forced to read in character, making sure both girls can see the pictures and making sure that I do not skip any words.

"Mommy, you're not reading the whole page," Mallory says, turning the page back to the previous one. "And I can't see the pictures very well," she says, trying to reposition herself on the arm of the rocking chair in Chloe's room.

"Sweetie, the meaning is the same. I just shortened it a little. Mommy is tired, I have a lot to do."

"How am I ever going to learn to read if you skip words?" she says, looking up at me with her big brown eyes. She has a point. I don't know. Isn't that what school is for?

The rushing doesn't end when the workweek ends. Our weekends are so crammed with activities and birthday parties that we race from one thing to another like bikers in the Tour de France. I also cram a couple of errands into the mix—just because I can.

"Okay, girls—first tennis lessons, then the dry cleaner, the grocery store, the pharmacy, and then Michael's birthday party, sound like fun?" They just stare at me from the backseat. I imagine they're wondering what it would be like to have a different mommy, a laid-back mommy. Sometimes I wonder what it would be like to *be* laid-back. I feel a little guilty about this, but then I think surely later in life they will benefit from learning to multitask at an early age.

The extent to which my rushing had rubbed off on my girls hit home when Mallory received her first kindergarten report card. Where we live, elementary school students are graded on a 1-to-4 scale, with 4 being exceptional. I was very proud when Mallory received all 4s and 3s on her first report card. Her teacher, Mrs. K, complimented Mallory in many areas, writing in the report card that she has "higher-order thinking skills," boasts "many friends," and is a "leader" in group activities.

I knew Mallory was smart—that was never a question or concern for me; she was a chip off the old block. I gave myself a little pat on the back for giving my oldest daughter the academic gene. Yes, the DNA from my family was shining through. I was always a good student. My husband was not. So clearly, I had the right to take credit for Mallory's brilliance. But even brilliance has a dark side. I read on.

Mrs. K also wrote that Mallory "often rushes through her work," making "careless errors." She said Mallory has so much "potential" but needs to slow down. At our first parent-teacher conference, she said Mallory was up and out of her seat turning in her assignment before other kids had chosen which pencil to use.

"Is there anyone in your family who is a list maker? Because Mallory is a real checklist girl, she likes to check things off, get things done fast, really fast," Mrs. K says in her soothing Mary Poppins tone. She has a serenity that only a character in a fairy tale could match.

Grif is now rolling his eyes and kicking my ankles under the table. There's no question where she gets her rushing gene. We both know I'm the guilty party.

"Well, I guess," I stammer, "truth be told I'm a little type A, and well, I don't know, maybe she got that from me?" I feel all my pride draining out onto the floor and pooling around my feet.

"*A little*," Grif says with more emphasis than I think is really necessary. "Mrs. K, she is so type A it's scary. She has definitely passed this on to Mallory." He crosses his arms and looks at me smugly.

"Well, I think you both [meaning me and Mallory, I assume] need to slow down," Mrs. K says with the authority of every teacher I've had in my whole entire life. I'm immediately back in first grade, forty-seven pounds with thick glasses, listening to Mrs. Trotter tell me the very same thing.

I nod and then realize she expects me to answer verbally. "Yes, ma'am, I will, we will try to concentrate more on slowing down, I promise."

And I mean it. I'm going to get a 4 in kindergarten if it kills me.

## PLAY-DOH FROM SCRATCH

Intellectually, we all know that we can only do so much, we have to prioritize, but somehow on the way to ballet while you're reading your e-mail on your Blackberry with one hand at stoplights, common sense gets lost.

Thinking about what I've committed to often keeps me awake at night. I lie in bed dead tired with lists and sublists going through my mind. This is a state of being that cannot be cured with Benadril or red wine. It will only stop if people stop asking me for things or I start saying no. What a concept, that I might actually say no to something.

> I will not make Play-Doh. I don't even cook for my family, why in the hell would I make frigging Play-Doh?

"No," I say with absolute authority to the preschool teacher, "I will not make Play-Doh. I don't even cook for my family, why in the hell would I make frigging Play-Doh? And while we're talking about it, why in God's name would anyone make something you can buy anyway? I mean, how expensive could the stuff be? It's colored dough, not crack."

Of course, I don't say any of this. I just politely write in my name on the line next to October. Then I go to Target and buy as much Play-Doh as I can carry because I feel guilty about not making it.

"Carol," one of the mothers says as she sees me with an armload of Play-Doh, "did you know that you could buy Play-Doh? I had no idea!"

. . . . . . . . . . . . . . . . . . . . . . . . . . . . . . . . . . . . . . .

## WHERE ARE YOUR COOKBOOKS?

Not cooking is another thing that earns me a fair amount of criticism amongst my peer group. One of my friends told me that no matter how late she gets home from work, she sits down at the dinner table with her family for a meal, a meal that she has prepared the night before. Not being someone who likes to be outdone, I tried this for a month. I set my clock for 5:00 a.m. and prepared the meal in the morning. After about a month of everyone pushing their plates away and saying they didn't like what I had cooked, I wisely gave it up.

So I solved the problem and at the same time minimized the chaos in my life by hiring an afternoon nanny who cooks dinner for my children—and leaves leftovers for us. Of course now I feel guilty about needing outside help with my children. That's the way it goes.

When Erin first started, I filled my refrigerator with a lot of easily prepared kid food— hot dogs, macaroni and cheese, chicken nuggets, fish sticks, pretty much the entire food pyramid that I was familiar with. After a couple of days, she politely asked me if she could cook some real dishes for the kids. I was thrilled and a little embarrassed by what I had been feeding them. Sure, why not, I thought. They've never had real food, but why not give it a try?

"I looked for your cookbooks," she tells me over the phone one day.

"My cookbooks?" I reply nervously. Clearly, the gig was up. The emperor really has no clothes.

"I don't have any," I say quietly into the receiver.

"Oh," she says and then pauses for what seems like four minutes, even though it was really about four seconds.

"That's okay," she rebounds cheerfully. "I have some; I'll look up some recipes and e-mail you some ideas."

The truth is at one time in my life I did own cookbooks. People had given them to me as gifts over the years. They came from people who didn't know me very well, or from well-intentioned people who hoped the cookbooks would jump-start my cooking career. They just sat there, taking up cabinet space, gathering dust. Every once in a while I would come across them and think, *Maybe I will make mandarin chicken or beef Wellington.* But I was fooling myself. I knew that I was never going to measure, dice, or sauté.

I think the day when I finally marked 25 cents on the cover of each book at a yard sale was one of the most freeing days of my life. I would not let them sit there on my shelf and mock me anymore. I was done with them.

"You're really getting rid of this?" a middle-aged woman with jeans pulled up just under her breasts asks me.

"Yes, I am. Good price. Got a lot of good recipes out of that one, lot of good years," I say, flabbergasted to be pulling out the hard sell for a quarter. Obviously I'm a yard sale whore, but that's another chapter, possibly another book.

"Why are you selling it?" she asks as she adjusts her bulging, black leather fanny pack on her hip.

"Why?" I say incredulously, wondering why someone has the gall to question my thought process about unloading junk at a yard sale. "Why? Because, well, the truth is I don't cook."

I had bared my soul to a complete stranger, Mrs. Highpants, standing in my cul-de-sac at 7:30 a.m. on a Saturday morning, and it felt *good*.

. . . . . . . . . . . . . . . . . . . . . . . . . . . . . . . . . . . . . . . . . .

## PERFECT HOUSE

Guilt is not always about work or the kids; often guilt is about what else is not getting done, like cleaning your house.

B.K.—before kids—I was a bit obsessive-compulsive about keeping my house neat. Grif, who is not afflicted with the neat-gene, quickly fell into lockstep with my tidiness plan soon after we were married. I think it was less about him liking a neat house and more about him not liking my bitching. For me to leave a bed unmade or a dish in the sink B.K. would have meant I was drunk or spiraling downward into mental illness.

> After kids—everything changed. I watched my once-neat house become a cesspool of dirt and disorganization.

But A.K.—after kids—everything changed. I watched my once-neat house become a cesspool of dirt and disorganization.

I asked my friend Molly one time what had to go after she had her second child. "Making beds," she said. "I just have no time to do it between work and everything else."

Her answer honestly caused me to have heart palpitations. Obviously, there was a whole new frontier for me to conquer trying to balance kids with my obsessive-compulsive tendencies.

Before I continue, I need to explain that the whole thing is my mother's fault. I know a lot of people say this about their shortcomings, vices, crazy tendencies . . . but for real, *it's her fault.*

From a very young age, I remember my mother alphabetizing spices (even though she didn't cook), making sure the zippers on the throw pillows were always turned in the same direction, and ensuring the carpets always had recent vacuum cleaner indentations.

Even now, as an adult, when I visit her house, it's as if I'm staying in a hotel, *a very, very clean hotel* with maids who are well paid. She has French linens on the bed in my room, and I'm not supposed to bend them. Sleeping without bending covers is an impossibility. So I lie there, very still, trying not to move too much. If I do get up in the morning to go to the bathroom and then head groggily back to bed, I find the bed has already been made. My mother, the bed-making fairy, swept in while I was taking my seven-second pee and somehow made the French-linen bed to perfection.

If you read part of the newspaper at her house and leave it on a table for a second, it is immediately put into the recycling bin. The newspaper fairy has swooped in to get that nasty, unruly newspaper off of the coffee table before it takes over the entire den.

If you drink out of a glass, leave it on her counter for a minute, and walk away, when you return, it's gone, vanished. The glass fairy slipped in when you weren't looking and slipped that dirty glass right into the dishwasher.

You see the pattern. In my case, the obsessive-compulsive gene is both hereditary and learned. Although my condition is not nearly as severe as my mother's (my husband might disagree with this), it still causes me a great deal of consternation.

A.K., I have loosened up a little, not by choice but by necessity. My house is still neat. I do make the beds, clean the dishes, and pick up the junk—but it's dirty as hell. And I feel guilty about this. For a moment, and then the moment passes.

For example, we have cream-colored carpeting in our bedrooms and a cream area rug in the den. Under low light they look fine, but it's got to be *really low light*. My couches are not much better. I got to the point where I could no longer turn the cushions over to hide the stains. Between pee, spilled milk, and Magic Markers, they look like a Salvador Dali painting and smell like a landfill.

But the best examples of my slackness as a housekeeper are the walls in the back hallway leading to the bedrooms. When Mallory was young, I learned that you *never* let small children have unsupervised access to Magic Markers. She completely covered a wall in the corner of my kitchen with doodles. Apparently, when Chloe came along, I developed amnesia because once again I am faced with childish handiwork, this time covering an entire wall.

As my tired brain processed what was happening, I said, "Chloe, why are you drawing with a yellow highlighter on the wall?"

"It's fun," she said, her finger clenched tightly around the highlighter. "Isn't it pretty, Mommy?"

I thought about painting the hallway, but I keep thinking I need to wait until she gets through the wall-drawing stage. At the rate we're going she might have a driver's license before she grows out of it. The other day I caught her drawing on the wall with a red pencil.

"Chloe, what are you doing?" I tried to wrestle the pencil from her pudgy fingers.

"Art, I'm making art."

And you know what I did? I let her keep on drawing. I let her create art.

. . . . . . . . . . . . . . . . . . . . . . . . . . . . . . . . . . . . . . . . . . . . . . .

## GIVING IN

I think the most tangible sign of a mother's guilt is giving in to what we really don't want to do. Whether it's giving them candy before dinner or allowing them to watch SpongeBob when you just can't take the whining anymore, we all do it. Sure, there are those perfect mothers who never raise their voices or allow their children to eat sugar, but they're not my friends, so I don't really care what they think of me.

For those women who think they are perfect, I have some advice. Let loose, go ahead, try it, you might like it. Throw the kids some chicken nuggets, let them stay up until ten, watch a PG movie with them, let them wear cowboy boots to church. I promise they'll survive and so will you.

> I told her yes, of course she could ride the bus someday. Well, someday is here and I'm not happy about it.

Recently, Mallory and I had a standoff over riding the school bus. Ever since she was a small child, the school bus has held magical significance. We would pull up behind a big yellow bus with flashing lights at an intersection, and she would gaze out the window in wonderment.

"Mommy, someday I am going to ride a bus like that one, right?" she would say with a certain wistfulness in her voice.

I told her yes, of course she could ride the bus someday. Well, someday is here and I'm not happy about it.

My first concern was safety. We all know who rides the bus—boys like Tommy Newton who threw chewed bubble gum at me when I was in third grade. It landed right on the top of my head. My mother cut it out because she wasn't clued in to the domestic wisdom about getting it out with ice. I had a piece of hair sticking up on top of my head for months. Tommy Newton naturally teased me about my new hairstyle. I hated Tommy Newton and therefore, in turn, I hated the bus.

The bus is also where I heard my first bad words. Clearly, the bus driver has her hands full. She can't spend her time monitoring the vulgar language of kids who take the opportunity to flex their potty-mouth muscles. I distinctly remember hearing the words "blow job" on the school bus. I had no idea what it meant, but apparently someone had given someone else one for a dollar in the back of the bus—not that I believe that for a second, now that I'm familiar with the term. Especially not for a mere dollar. Anyway, I'm really not ready to explain this stuff to my six-year-old.

But she wore me down. Mallory has a way of doing that. She repeats her pleas over and over again until I break like a suspect in an interrogation room. Somewhere in between Mallory's guttural screams and the desperate explanations that her life would not be complete without riding the school bus, I did what every parent who wants sanity does. I gave in.

The first week of school alone I think I wasted about seven hours of my life waiting at the stupid bus stop. I'm so terrified that she might, God forbid, miss the bus and hold me responsible that I get out there extra early to make sure this doesn't happen. I could feel my life slipping away as I sat on the corner ticking through in my mind all the tasks I needed to complete. Not much can be done at the bus stop while I'm trying to keep Chloe from jumping off the curb into traffic. Every time a yellow bus came up, I leapt up and squinted, looking for the number, praying it's 1139.

"There it is," I shouted.

"No, Mommy," she said, with her arms crossed, "that's not it. That's bus 225. Can't you see the number? When is my bus going to come?"

That, of course, was the million-dollar question. Everyone seems to know the first week of school is plagued by transportation problems. But, this being my first foray into being a bus mom, I had no idea how much inconsistency and waiting the process involved. I'm a very bad waiter. I pretty much eschew all activities that involve lines or waiting. If I am *forced* to wait, I always try to have something with me to read. But unfortunately, the bus stop situation requires my full attention—which pisses me off.

The first day the bus never showed up, so I drove Mallory and her friend to school so they wouldn't be late.

As a result, Chloe was late for her first day of ballet. Chloe was adorable in her big sister's hand-me-down ballet outfit, but there was one very important thing missing—ballet shoes. The teacher shook her head vigorously at Chloe's little pink sneakers. So I rushed Chloe into class in her stocking feet and ran down the hallway to the ballet school store to purchase overpriced ballet shoes. Grif would have run to Wal-Mart, but there was no time—my kid was running around on slippery hardwood floors in stocking feet.

"Are you sure you don't want to try them on?" the saleswoman asked. I'm sure she is used to more discerning mothers who try things on and comparison-shop before they make a decision. I'd be just as happy to buy everything I need on the Internet, from groceries to underwear, and have it delivered to my door.

"I'm sure," I said and plunked down my credit card. Shoes in hand, I ran back toward the class.

Chloe was on her stomach stretching in a circle with seven other three-year-olds. I had to contort my body in a very inappropriate manner, one where I'm sure my thong underwear was sticking out of my shorts, while I struggled to put the little ballet slippers on her fat little feet. I could feel the eyes of the mothers behind me boring a hole in my back, wondering why God had allowed me to procreate.

> I could feel the eyes of the mothers behind me boring a hole in my back, wondering why God had allowed me to procreate.

Later that same day I met Mallory at the bus stop after school and asked the driver what time she would normally be coming in the morning. She thumbed through the paperwork on her lap and said 9:00. *9:00*, I thought, *this is insane.* Being the rational person that I am, I immediately pegged this as reverse discrimination against an upper-middle-class, neighborhood. I imagined transportation department administrators deciding that women with manicured lawns, minivans, and middle-of-the-day Pilates classes wouldn't mind a 9:00 bus pickup time. If *some* neighborhood was going to get the late bus, it was going to be ours.

There was no such grand conspiracy, but I was energized. I had a raging desire to get things changed. After many calls to transportation managers and the principal, I discovered there was simply a shortage of bus drivers, and my driver had several routes to deal with before ours. So I told Mallory I would need to drop her off at school in the morning because the bus was coming too late for me to get to work on time.

Cue the guilt trip.

"I wish you didn't work," she screamed, her plump lips forming the perfect follow-up pout, her brow furrowed and her arms crossed tightly. I could tell she meant business. "I really, really, *really* want to take the bus," she wailed, stomping her foot for emphasis.

"Well, I *do* work, and 9:00 is an unreasonable time for a bus to come anyway. How do they think anyone who works can deal with that?" I crossed *my* arms and stomped *my* foot. Again, I was trying to use adult logic with a six-year-old; clearly, I am not right in the head, as Southerners are prone to say about crazy people.

"I don't care if you're late for work," she bellowed, "I want to ride the bus!"

"Okay," I said, uncrossing my arms.

"Okay? Really? But won't you get fired if you're late every day?" And then she smiled.

"Maybe, but at least you'll be happy," I said, beaten down once again by guilt. "I'll work it out."

And I meant it, because somehow I always do.

· · · · · · · · · · · · · · · · · · · · · · · · · · · · · · · · · · · · · ·

## YOU PLAY, YOU PAY

Another thing that provokes guilt in most mothers is doing anything for yourself. I'm not talking about fancy stuff like going to a spa. I'm talking about running to Target or going to a movie with a girlfriend. These simple acts can be enough to send your children into full-blown fallout tantrums—likely to include hateful words that sound like they're coming from someone who is possessed.

"Mommy, why do you always have to leave? I don't like you!" Mallory says, slamming her body onto the hardwood floor in the hallway and scrunching up her face. At the same time, Chloe is holding onto my leg and I'm dragging her toward the door.

"Girls, I'm just going to Target," I say, reaching for the door handle. "Stay and play with Daddy, I'll be back in an hour."

"You're dressed nice," Mallory says suspiciously. She's on to me. She is now propped up on her elbows on the floor beneath my legs. "I think you're going somewhere else."

My children are used to seeing me in work clothes, which usually means a suit, or workout clothes, which I wear whenever I am with them on my days off. So when they see me in jeans and a cute top, they know something is up. Damn girls— if I had boys they would never even notice.

"Well, Mommy is going to meet Miss Cathy after Target, just for an appetizer, not a full dinner, just a few minutes. I promise," I say, trying to defend my outing, negotiating with small terrorists again. Haven't I learned anything about their sly manipulations, their tactics?

"Then you're going to be longer than an hour," Mallory wails, grabbing onto my other leg.

Luckily, I've been fortunate enough to build up a stable of good babysitters. For some reason my girls don't whine as much when I leave them with their father or a *fun* babysitter. With their Daddy they get to do cool stuff like ride on the John Deere, watch *Dirty Harry*, eat popcorn for dinner, and play pool. But babysitters do crafts with them—something not at the top of my repertoire. Crafts are even better than riding on the John Deere.

I'm quite a babysitter networker. Anytime I meet a young girl, I ask her if she babysits. If she says something like, "I could," forget it. But if she answers enthusiastically, "I'd love to!" she's programmed right into the Blackberry. I rotate them, I pay well, and I always get the lowdown from Mallory so I know who not to invite back.

"I don't like her, Mommy," Mallory says.

"Why not?" I say, worried, imagining stories about someone who smokes pot in my house, raids my liquor cabinet, and has sex with her boyfriend in my bed while my children watch an R-rated movie in the den.

"She's just not very fun, she doesn't talk much, and she doesn't do crafts."

"Well, that's it, I'm deleting her," I say, my finger already scrolling through the contacts for her name.

The big problem parents get into is trying to combine their fun and their children's fun. This is clearly prompted and perpetuated by the guilt of leaving them behind. You feel like you can have more fun if your children are also having fun. Where did this come from? My parents never cared whether I had fun when they went out. They left me with Denise, who smoked in the bathroom, drank their vodka, and talked on the telephone to her boyfriend all night. She usually let us stay up late, watch *Creature Double Feature*, and eat ice cream with chocolate sauce as long as we didn't tell on her. Yes, we were in good hands.

With their Daddy they get to do cool stuff like ride on the John Deere, watch *Dirty Harry*, eat popcorn for dinner, and play pool.

In a misguided effort to combine my enjoyment with my children's, I organize gatherings that involve friends and their children. We feed the kids first and then let them play while we eat in the dining room and consume many bottles of wine. During one recent dinner we were acting like total rednecks, letting the kids destroy the house, stay up late, and eat anything they wanted. At one point I was looking for Chloe after a long period of not seeing her running through the dining room in a cape pulling a wooden Dalmatian on a leash.

"Chloe, where are you?" I yelled through my red-wine haze, hoping that she hadn't decided to leave the house.

"Here, Mommy," she said in a muffled voice. I found her crouched behind the couch. Her two-year-old little friend, a boy she calls Rachel because she can't pronounce his real name, Marshall, was hurling tennis balls at her across the room.

"Are you okay?" I asked.

"Having fun," she laughed and ducked to avoid another ball, which hit me in the shoulder.

"Okay, well, don't break anything," I said, patting her on the back and holding my head down to get out of the line of fire.

One perfect summer evening I was invited to attend an outdoor Earth, Wind and Fire concert with forty friends who rented a bus. Grif was out of town, so I planned to bring my girls to my friend's house and we would hire one babysitter for the evening. Then we would all spend the night, which meant I wouldn't have to drive. From the beginning this plan had red flags popping up everywhere, but in my funky, summertime, Amstel Light–fueled mind-set, I ignored them.

The concert was amazing. We danced until we were overcome with sweat and $9 stadium beers. Around 2:00 a.m. I slipped into my friend's guest room and got into bed with Mallory. Chloe was sleeping in her pack-and-play at the foot of the bed. I lay there congratulating myself on what a great plan I had engineered. The girls had a blast with their friends Kathryn and Elizabeth, I had a blast at the concert, and now I was sleeping with my girls harmoniously in one bedroom. Imagine that! I'm glad I had at least five minutes to bask in the joy of this glorious moment, because as quickly as it came, it ended.

At about 2:15 a.m. Chloe woke up. I was afraid she would wake my friends, so I pulled her into bed with us. Minutes later she woke up Mallory. The two of them started to play, fight, roll around, giggle, and generally force me into immediate hangover mode where I didn't think I could take one more second of their antics. I had made my bed, literally. I had chosen to play, and now it was obvious that I was going to pay.

I considered getting up and leaving, but I remembered that my friend's car was parked behind mine. I was trapped. So the torture, and I do mean *torture*, went on for several hours until I heard my friend's husband get up to walk the dog. Like a woman possessed, I raced out into the hall and urgently asked him to move his car.

I threw our belongings into a duffel bag, quickly made the bed, and marched the girls to the car, barefoot, in their pajamas. They walked in silence. Clearly, they knew what they had done, but I think they harbored no guilt because, unlike adults, they waste no energy on guilt.

As we climbed into the car, the sun was just starting to peek over the horizon, casting an orange glow on my windshield. In my rearview mirror I caught a glimpse of their little tired faces bathed in the warm, orange glow. From this angle they did look a little bit contrite. And I thought maybe I was being too hard on them. They can't help acting like little crazy people at times; that's what kids do.

"Girls, how about we all climb in Mommy's bed and watch a movie when we get home," I said. "I love you guys, you know that, right? Mommy is sorry for getting mad."

"Love you, too," Mallory said, lazily closing her eyes as the early-morning sun blinded her.

Chloe was already asleep, her mouth wide open and a hand propping up her little chin.

hat's Sex Got to Do with It?

*"You cannot shake hands
with a clenched fist."*
—Indira Gandhi

Relationships are funny things. In the beginning they are about the two people living in a vacuum where nothing else, nobody else, exists. They are about love, lust, excitement. And then, all of a sudden, without warning, they become something else all together. They become defined by bills, a mortgage, children, family, holidays, friends, car payments, vacations. In other words, they no longer exist in the vacuum where new relationships first take root, grow, and flourish. They morph into something that is much bigger than just the two people who started the whole thing in the first place. This metamorphosis makes them, in roughly equal measure, difficult to leave and hard to tolerate.

   One of the first things to go in any marriage that is child-centered is sex. Let's face it, who has the time or energy for sex? I mean, you might as well be asking me if I want to go out and run ten miles if you approach me about sex anytime after 10:00 p.m. It's like this. I could have sex, or I could take a bath and read *People* magazine. I could have sex, or I could snuggle up under my comforter and watch *American Idol*. It's not that I don't like sex; it's that after being awake for seventeen hours, I'm like a dead car battery that not even jumper cables can resuscitate.

## THE GARBAGE INCIDENT

Besides the exhaustion, there are the little things about your guy that fester. There's the fact that he leaves his dirty underwear hanging on a hook near the shower. There's the fact that he leaves his dirty cereal bowl in the sink every day. There's the fact that he never makes the bed, any bed, when you make three every day. These little annoyances build up inside you until it's impossible to think about sex with this person.

Men, I suspect, have no such barriers to sex. For them it's like eating a good burger or having a cold beer; *anytime, anywhere,* is how I think most men think about sex. They don't attach it to emotional baggage like women do. Maybe this is healthier. I don't know. I'll never know because I'm a woman and when I'm pissed off, which is most of the time, he's not getting any, period.

We had an impromptu dinner party for close friends one early fall evening. There were eight adults, six kids (including two babies), lots of food, wine, and laughter. It was a wonderful night, the kind of unplanned, unexpected moment in time that feeds your soul with warm, fuzzy feelings for days to come.

After everyone left, we started the cleanup, a process that had been started by well-meaning guests but would ultimately be our responsibility into the wee hours. At one point Grif came up from the garage and told me that our twelve-year-old Sheltie, Max, had ripped open a garbage bag and spread trash all over the garage. He told me it was my fault for putting the bag in a place that the dog could get to it. So, after everything I had done to make the evening a great success—bought the food, cleaned the house, set the table—it all came down to the garbage.

"You're just like those people I deal with at work. I have to babysit them," he said, referring to his minimum-wage employees at the scrap yard that he runs.

It was the word *babysit* that really set me off, because I manage every aspect of Grif's life out of work: the house, the children, our social life, every last detail.

Needless to say, I refused to clean up the garbage and so did he. It became a negotiating tool.

"Okay, I'll clean up the playroom if you clean up the garbage," I'd say.

"Forget it," he'd say. "I'll do it myself. But one thing I'm definitely not doing is cleaning up the garbage."

The garbage almost became a euphemism for our marriage. For all I know, by the time you read this, the garbage will still be sitting there in my garage—decomposing food, smelly diapers, scraps of paper, shred and spread in every direction. By now it's probably covered in maggots and maybe even attracting rats (if they exist in our little pristine suburb). The truth is, no one is having sex until someone cleans up the garbage.

## CAN'T TOUCH THIS

Another issue with mothers and sex is that mothers have children crawling all over them all the time. The last thing they want is someone else, namely their husbands, crawling all over them.

From breastfeeding on, children need a certain amount of physical contact with their mothers every day. This can be a joy. Sometimes. Other times, it makes me want to live like John Travolta in

*The Boy in the Plastic Bubble.* Sure, people could reach in the bubble with those big rubber gloves and simulate touching him, but it was too dangerous to actually touch him. He rolled around in that plastic bubble all day long. He could see and hear people, but there was absolutely no touching. I could get used to that.

When Chloe crawls into bed, she immediately attaches to me like an octopus.

I remember breastfeeding Chloe for just two months before I had a breakdown on my parents' deck at the Jersey Shore. Out of the blue, I stood up and made an announcement in front of my entire family.

"See these big boobs, people?" I said, as everyone looked up from their newspapers and magazines with that here-we-go-again-she's-losing-it look. "Take a good look because this is the last day you're going to see these puppies; they're going away. I'm done, I'm taking my body back, and I'm taking it back starting right this minute."

While breastfeeding is simply a distant nightmare to me now, I still deal with unwanted touch. Chloe has a habit of coming into our bed around 5:00 in the morning. I never allowed this with Mallory, but now I'm frankly just too old and too tired to fight it. When Chloe crawls into bed, she immediately attaches to me like an octopus. She throws one leg across my waist and shoves the other one beneath my butt. She wraps one arm around my neck in a viselike grip and, with the other hand, strokes my hair in what she thinks is a loving manner.

One could look at these moments as precious mother-daughter time, fleeting expressions of love between a child and parent that are to be treasured. I see it as manipulation. What Chloe *really* wants is for me to get up, turn on cartoons, and fix her breakfast. After about fifteen minutes of her elbow in my ribs and her pulling out individual strands of my hair, I give in.

By the time Grif leans over on a Friday night after a few beers and starts pawing my hair in the same manner that Chloe does, I am done giving in.

"Leave me alone," I say. "I just want to be in my plastic bubble."

. . . . . . . . . . . . . . . . . . . . . . . . . . . . . . . . . . . . . . . .

## DATE NIGHT

To combat the doldrums of marriage, many couples have adopted the concept of *date night*. This phrase makes me think of housewives in the '50s who met their husbands at the door with a gin and tonic, slippers, and a pipe.

In my house I'm the one who comes home last. Instead of a hot bath and a glass of wine, I'm met at the door with dirty (literally from head to toe) children, who jump on me the second my foot hits the threshold. Sometimes they knock me down because I can't balance their total weight—ninety pounds—in my impossibly high heels. If I dare to look around, I see the hurricane that my family has left in its wake—shoes, coats, book bags, mail. It's as if some magnetic force has stripped them of their belongings when they stepped into the hallway, and an invisible force field makes them powerless to pick things up and put them away.

> To me *date night* sounds about as exciting as *meat loaf night.*

To me *date night* sounds about as exciting as *meat loaf night*. There are a lot of other phrases that I think would be much more appealing. For example, *expensive restaurant night,*

*R-rated movie night, three-martini night.* But no, we insist on keeping it so Ozzie-and-Harriet that it loses its appeal.

Babysitters are so expensive that a night out with Grif usually ends with us trying to beat the lights so we can make it home by 11:00 and not have to pay for another half hour.

"How much do we owe her now?" Grif asks nervously, his hands gripping the steering wheel tightly, his eyes scanning the intersection in front of us for cars. I can tell he's thinking of running the light. I'm thinking about it, too. It's late. Nobody is around in our sleepy little suburb. Who would know?

"Forty, but if we don't make this light it's going to be an extra five," I say, picturing a Dukes of Hazzard move where our Volvo sails through the intersection and takes flight just as we round the curve on the other side.

. . . . . . . . . . . . . . . . . . . . . . . . . . . . . . . . . . . . . . . . . . .

## CLEAN GETAWAY

For couples stuck in a bigger rut than the date-night couples, there is the *weekend getaway.* But in truth this requires a heroic amount of planning. A babysitter must be lined up. Detailed instructions for the caregiver must be left, covering everything from breakfast to bedtime. Clothes must be laid out, meals planned, emergency numbers posted. By the time you get to your weekend getaway, all you want to do is sleep.

"Do you want to have sex?" I ask.

"Not really," he says. "I'm kind of tired."

"Me too," I say, stifling a yawn.

When you have young children, sleep is such a precious commodity that it usually wins out over sex. Sadly, you go from *I can't believe we didn't have sex this week* to *when was the last time I had sex?*

But you don't ask these questions on your weekend get-away. There are so many other things you want to do that you never get to do when you're with your children—eat a meal in peace, pee by yourself, try on clothes without someone crawling under the dressing room door, and exercise without interruption (my exercise at home gets put on hold often for butt-wiping—Chloe's, not mine). There simply aren't enough hours in the day for sex.

## SPIN THE BOTTLE

Mallory is just now beginning to understand the concept of boy-girl interactions. When we watch a Lifetime movie together, for example, she wants to know why the heroine is kissing more than one man throughout the story.

"Mommy, why is that lady kissing *him*?" Mallory says, her brown eyes bulging. "They're not married, are they? Isn't she married to the other guy that she was kissing before?"

These are questions I did not think I would have to answer until much later in life. But it's a different world today.

> I told her that only married people kissed and that you had to be thirty by law to have a baby.

Apparently, somewhere along the line, I told her that only married people kissed and that you had to be thirty by law to have a baby. She took every word to heart.

"Mommy, there's this girl in my class, Mary, she's my age and her mother is *twenty-four*! I did the math, Mommy, how can that be right?"

"Well, it's biologically possible to have children at a younger age than thirty, but it's not a very good idea," I say, wondering if a six-year-old has a bullshit detector. I try not to meet her eyes so that she can't bust me.

She asks, "Well, the reason to wait is you're supposed to know someone a long time before you get married and have kids, right?"

"Right, that's right," I say wholeheartedly.

"How long did you know Daddy before you got married?"

"Uh," I hesitate. "About two years."

"Do you really think that's long enough?" she asks with her hands on her hips. "I mean, he leaves a lot of stuff on the floor and he doesn't listen very well."

"That's true, Baby, very true," I say, wondering if maybe she's onto something.

· · · · · · · · · · · · · · · · · · · · · · · · · · · · · · · · · · · · · · · · ·

# IF THEY CAN'T MAKE IT...

I learned a long time ago that you should not look to famous people for inspiration in your marriage. The average marriage in Hollywood seems to last anywhere from three weeks to three years. Understanding this concept of short-term marriages among the rich and famous, my husband and I have always shared a little joke about the demise of their relationships.

"Oh no, Honey, it's official, Justin Timberlake and Cameron Diaz are done, caput, over," I yell from the tub as I page through my moist magazine.

"You're kidding," he feigns shock from his indentation on the mattress where he is performing his usual ritual of channel-surfing and dozing.

"If *they* can't make it . . ." I say, pausing strategically.

"Who can?" he says, finishing the sentence we've repeated so many times it's almost not funny anymore.

We also take delight in the coupling of celebrities with a track record of short marriages followed by in-your-face public divorces.

"Did you hear, Sweetie, they finally did it, those crazy kids," I say. "Pamela Anderson and Kid Rock, they tied the knot." I'm on my lawn chair by the neighborhood pool, flipping through a dog-eared magazine and occasionally checking to make sure the kids are not drowning. My cold beer is cleverly disguised in a hugger with the name of my bank on it.

"You don't say. Now there's a relationship that's going to *last*," he says, stuffing another cookie in his mouth, dropping crumbs all over his chest.

But really, why can't they make it? I mean, most relationships fail because people don't have the time and energy to invest in them. But the way I see it, rich and famous people should have nothing but time and energy. They have people who clean for them, cook for them, take care of their children; I mean, they could be having sex all day long. So what's the problem? The only thing I can figure is that all that time spent on movie sets with hot costars gives them totally unrealistic expectations of what marriage is supposed to be. Lucky for me I have no such fantasies.

. . . . . . . . . . . . . . . . . . . . . . . . . . . . . . . . . . . . . . . . . . . . . . . .

## BUY THE BOOK

One time in my I'm-going-to-bring-the-romance-back-into-my-life phase, I bought a book called *The Great American Sex Diet* by Laura Corn. It got great reviews on Amazon.com. Readers promised that it would "renew my sex life" and bring it to "unimaginable heights." A man named David in the book was quoted as saying, "A romp solves all sorts of problems." I was

Imagine that, a book that could turn a prude into a naked-doorway-waver. I had to have it.

like "Amen, David," a man after my own heart.

Surprisingly, the book was also reviewed on NPR, where readers called in and shared its wisdom. I especially enjoyed one anecdote from a man who said that, after reading the book, his wife stood in their front door naked and waved to him as he left for work every morning. Apparently, this daily peep show was enough to sexually jump-start this particular marriage for an entire year. I like the image of the naked woman in the doorway waving at her husband as he backs the pickup truck down the driveway, a grin on his face. I also imagine the neighbors' husbands all deciding to pull out of their driveways at the same time. This woman was apparently prudish before she read the book. Imagine that, a book that could turn a prude into a naked-doorway-waver. I had to have it.

When the book arrived in the mail, I told Grif about it and placed it prominently next to the bed.

"Come on, just one chapter," the pretty red cover seemed to call out to me. "I can *help* you. I have the *power*."

Somehow, I thought that by simply placing the book next to my bed, it would stimulate us. I thought that maybe by it being so close to the bed, it would leak through osmosis into our brains at night while we were sleeping. Apparently books don't work that way. You actually have to *read* them.

So, after weeks of staring at the book next to my bed and feeling guilty about not reading it, I finally put it away in a cabinet.

It sits there beneath a pile of other books I intend to read. But one crazy night, who knows, I might actually pull it out and read it. The next morning, if you're lucky, you might see me naked at the front door, waving goodbye to my husband.

# Jogging to Freedom

*"You can't be brave if you've only had wonderful things happen to you."*
—Mary Tyler Moore

For most mothers the word *freedom* is about as elusive as sex after marriage. You spend your days trying to figure out how to get it. You are jealous of people who have more of it than you do, and want to know how they got it.

"Angie gets to go out on Saturday and do whatever she wants without the kids," I say to Grif as he circles rental homes in the classifieds that he will never buy. "She can go shopping, get a massage, whatever," I say, furiously stirring my coffee, hoping the clinking of the spoon against the side of the cup will awaken him. "Mike watches the kids while she's gone, all day."

"That's nice," Grif says, "I need to run to Home Depot." He jumps up from the table and grabs his wallet, keys, and phone from the kitchen counter.

This is why we need to create our own path to freedom. For me there's always been one vehicle that can get me there no matter how many hills I have to climb in the process—the baby jogger.

When I just had Mallory, I owned a single jogger. This allowed me to take long walks despite the terrain. Like a four-wheel-drive vehicle, the jogger can jump curbs and go off-road. Eventually, it became a means for me to start running again.

When Chloe came along, I graduated to the famed double jogger. This cumbersome vehicle is wider than a rickshaw and more cumbersome than a wheelbarrow full of rocks, but it works. As a baby and a young toddler, Chloe needed to ride. Mallory needed to ride because she couldn't walk fast enough to keep up with me, and I couldn't stand her constant whining.

Every weekend my neighbor and I would load up our double baby joggers and stroll to the park. Of course we couldn't walk next to each other because the joggers take up the entire sidewalk, so we went single file and still managed to have some semblance of adult conversation.

"You know the lady who works at the toy store, the one in the wheelchair?" I bellow to my friend Libby, trying to be heard over the squeaky wheels. "She said she can get us that new chalk for the kids."

"Oh my God, she can walk?" Libby says. "That's amazing."

"No I said chalk, not walk. Never mind, I'll tell you later," I say, retreating into the monotonous sound of the squeaky wheels at my feet. So I can't hear, but at least I'm moving and not on the couch watching *Walker Texas Ranger* reruns.

## THE PRICE OF FREEDOM

"Daddy needs to see you in the driveway," Mallory said to me with an unusual level of urgency, the kind of urgency that someone who has bad news usually carries in her voice. I quickly got up from my deck chair at my dad's house.

I rounded the corner of the house and saw it immediately. It was a pile of mangled metal and canvas lying in a sad heap on the grass next to the driveway. The tires were flat as pancakes. Someone, or something, had crushed my double baby jogger and then left it there to die.

"Where did you leave the jogger?" Grif said, rocking Chloe in his arms with a knowing tone in his voice.

"I don't know," I said, still in shock.

"You don't know?"

> Someone, or something, had crushed my double baby jogger and then left it there to die.

I was starting to think it meant more to him than it did to me. But he was obviously assessing what it would cost to replace it. He knew it wasn't going to be cheap. Men and dollar signs.

"I guess I left it behind Dad's car," I said.

"You guess," he said in his best scolding tone as he jiggled Chloe on his shoulder.

What I couldn't figure out was how my father had flattened the baby jogger in his Lincoln Navigator and then simply taken off without a word. How could he not know that he hit it? This is a man with a Crackberry who calls me every five minutes to ask me the most mundane questions.

"Do you think two six packs of Dr Pepper will be enough for the week?" he calls to ask me.

"Enough for what, an all-nighter? Yes, Dad, that's fine," I say quickly before he abruptly moves on to a caller on his other line without saying goodbye.

"Do you know what your plans are for spring break yet?" he asks me during another twenty-second call.

"Dad, it's not even the end of the summer yet, no, I really haven't planned that far ahead," I say. Click, he's gone again.

So you would think someone with this much of an addiction to cell phones would call and give me a heads-up that he just crushed my baby jogger.

He might have called and said, "Hey, just wanted to let you know, crushed the jogger on the way to my meeting, we'll deal with it later. Love you."

But instead there was complete cell phone silence.

"So you didn't know you hit it?" I asked him later as we surveyed the twisted pile of metal in the grass. Like a crime scene, I left everything just the way he had left it. I imagined blocking it off with yellow tape while I waited for crime scene investigators to process the scene.

"I think it can be fixed," he said, trying to pry the crushed wheel back from the bent frame.

"I thought you had one of those things on that fancy car that beeps when you are backing into something," I said, trying to make eye contact with him.

"It doesn't always work," he said, pulling as hard as he could on the wheel. "Yeah, this definitely can be fixed."

Rex at the bike shop in town didn't look as sure as my dad did. In fact, he looked like he was going to tell us to send it to the baby jogger graveyard, but then I think he saw something in my eyes, something that told him he had to try. He stroked his beard and then ran his fingers through his long, stringy hair.

"Give me a couple of hours," Rex said with the confidence of a man who really thought he might win the lottery someday.

So my dad and I wandered in and out of shops, trying to kill time. He was uncharacteristically quiet. Finally, I just asked him. He was ducking behind a rack of clothes when I popped the question.

"You knew you hit it, didn't you?" I asked.

"I was in a hurry," he said, pretending to look at the price tag on a black slinky dress that wouldn't fit either one of us.

"Just admit it, I'm not mad, I put it there. I just need to know," I said. "Why didn't you just call and tell me?"

"I was late for my meeting," he said, obviously having rehearsed the answer in his head all day long. "Plus, I had to stop and get it after it spun out into traffic."

Turns out he not only hit it but also sent it careening into a four-lane road where people were forced to slam on brakes to avoid hitting it. The other drivers didn't know the jogger was empty. For all they knew it was carrying kids, which meant they might have hit something else in order to avoid the jogger. These other drivers narrowly missed the jogger before my dad grabbed it and pulled it onto the grass.

"It can be fixed," he said again with confidence. "If not, I'll get you another one."

# The Crazy House

*"Do not what you would undo if caught."*
—Leah Arendt

My children are trying to make me a better person, and it's really pissing me off.

Intellectually, I knew things would have to change when I had children, but emotionally, I was not prepared for this dramatic transformation. Cursing was the first vice to go. I finally dropped it for good (around the children, mind you) when my oldest daughter, Mallory, heard me use the F-word under my breath one day at a mere eighteen months old. She didn't repeat it immediately, but clearly she filed it away in her little baby brain. The next day we were playing a rhyming game, and she had to say a word that rhymed with *truck*. Unfortunately, she did not come up with *duck*. You get the picture.

Like little sponges, kids soak up everything we say and do, good and bad. One morning when Mallory was three she came down the stairs with her underwear wedged into the crack of her bottom. I asked her why she was wearing it that way and she said proudly, "I want to be like you, Mommy." I was horrified. Luckily, no one makes thongs for toddlers.

· · · · · · · · · · · · · · · · · · · · · · · · · · · · · · · · · · · · ·

## SHAKE IT LIKE YOU MEAN IT

At Mallory's first parent-teacher conference in kindergarten, I was told that she "danced inappropriately" during music time in the classroom. I flashed back to those nights teaching her to shake her groove thing to "I Will Survive" by Gloria Gaynor. My kids don't know a lot about nursery rhymes, but they know how to dance the heck out of a good funky disco tune. From "Brick House" to "Gold Digger" (the clean version), they undulate around the room until their little faces are bright red, their arms and legs flailing. Until recently, Chloe performed in a diaper. It's kind of like a rave in our den, only without drugs. Of course, being the involved, hands-on parent that I am, I not only eagerly participate, I guide.

"Come on, that's the best you can do?" I say to Mallory. "Shake it like you mean it, a little lower now; really get some hip into it."

"I'm trying, Mommy, I really am," she says, wiping the sweat from her brow and shaking her little hips.

I turn my attention to my youngest pupil. "Show me what you got, Chloe, you've got the floor," I say. "Okay, here comes the chorus, break it down."

"How's my booty look, Mama?" Chloe asks seriously.

"Real good, Baby, real good," I say, bursting with parental pride.

While other parents were doing the Little Teapot dance and The Hokey Pokey, I was essentially teaching my daughters how to dance like Vegas showgirls. In the long run, I figure it's a skill they can always fall back on.

. . . . . . . . . . . . . . . . . . . . . . . . . . . . . . . . . . . . . . .

## PASS THE SAUCE

One of the things I'm happy to report that my kids *haven't* picked up on is drinking alcohol. When Mallory was very little, she called wine "Mommy's juice." Now at six she calls it "Mommy's medicine," which, frankly, I think is pretty darn perceptive for a little kid. I've let her smell it before, and she thinks it smells disgusting. Chloe, on the other hand, would drink bong water if it were offered to her in a cup, so we don't leave errant glasses of alcohol around our house, lest we might end up with a drunken kid and a visit from social services.

I've also sheltered my kids from my all-time vice, soda. Okay, I'll admit it. I'm not ashamed. It's more specific than that. I'm a Pepper. I guess in reality I've been one my whole life, but now I've resigned myself to it. From the time I saw those corny people in the seventies singing *I'm a Pepper, wouldn't you like to be a Pepper too,* I was saying *yes, yes, I am a Pepper.* The truth is I need Dr Pepper to survive. For me, having my one delicious, sugar-filled, caffeine-infused cold beverage a day makes all of the difference in my ability to function.

But for my kids? No way. It's milk, water, or juice, in that order. I know they'll eventually get hooked on something. Maybe it will be vodka or maybe it will be Diet Coke, but I see no need to nudge them in that direction. It amazes me that parents allow their children to drink soda. For me, it's about sanity. The last thing I need is little wired people bouncing off the walls, craving their next caffeine fix.

I gave Chloe chocolate cake for the first time when she was two. It was what I imagine a two-year-old on crack might look like. She jumped off the couch onto the ottoman and pole-vaulted over me as I lay on the floor watching a movie. She ran manically up and down the hallway, her wisps of barely-a-head-of-hair standing on end as she pretty much bounced like a pinball from wall to wall.

. . . . . . . . . . . . . . . . . . . . . . . . . . . . . . . . . . . . . . . .

## PUT A SOCK IN IT

I have failed my children miserably in the edit-what-you-say category. I quickly got out of the habit of cursing in front of them, but I forget that there are still *other* things I shouldn't be saying. Somehow I still think of my kids as visitors from a foreign country who don't really understand what I say. I carry on adult conversations in the car on the cell phone, all of the time thinking they don't really understand what I'm saying. For some reason I can't get it through my head that they are hanging, literally hanging, on every word I say.

> Somehow I still think of my kids as visitors from a foreign country who don't really understand what I say.

"Mommy, what's a bitch?" Mallory asks after one such conversation.

"Well, Sweetie," I say, feeling my I'm-really-going-to-hell vibe kicking in. "It's when someone isn't nice. But it's a bad word. I didn't mean it. We don't use that word in our family. Mommy's sorry for saying it."

"It's okay, Mommy, I get it. Grandma is a bitch."

"Close, baby, Grandma *can be* a b-i-t-c-h, let's get it right." The scary thing is that it literally happened overnight.

They went from silent observers who might as well have been listening to Russian, to little spies who hear every word and file it away to be repeated at some later, completely inappropriate time.

When Mallory was a baby and I changed her diaper, I would say in a singsong voice, "Who has a stinky butt?" Apparently, I must have said it deep into toddlerhood because she took it on as one of her very favorite phrases. During church, when the children would go up to the altar for the children's sermon and sit at the minister's feet, I lived in fear that the phrase would come up as he passed the microphone around and asked the children questions.

"Now the wise men brought baby Jesus three gifts. Can anyone name one?" the minister says. Mallory's hand would always shoot up even if she didn't have an answer. She just liked to be called on. He held the microphone close to her mouth. I could hear her heavy breathing and then a muffled response. My heart dropped. I just knew it was going to be "stinky butt."

"Gold," she finally said in an audible voice. "Gold."

## WHAT LIES BENEATH

Adults tell little white lies practically every day. We tell ourselves that they are harmless and a necessary evil in modern society. But unlike us, kids see things in black and white. As far as they're concerned, there is no gray.

"No, you don't look fat in that dress," I say to a girlfriend who is stuffing an extra twenty pounds into a lime green silk number. But three-year-old Chloe routinely tells members of my family that they have big boobs and fat butts. She once told a woman in an elevator that she thought her butt might be too

SMOTHERHOOD

big to fit through the door. Luckily, the woman laughed. Chloe means no harm. She's just saying it like it is.

"I'm so sorry we can't make the party, we're going to be out of town," I say to a sometime-friend who has the most boring parties in the universe. I'll really be at home watching a movie and eating pizza.

"But, Mommy," Mallory says, "we're going on vacation next weekend, not *this* weekend."

"Oh, that's right," I say, feeling the red splotchy lie spots begin to creep up my neck. "I must have gotten the dates mixed up."

Kids see the world in absolutes. To them there is no such thing as a little lie; it's like being a little bit pregnant. You either are or you aren't. You're either lying or you're not.

One rainy afternoon I decided to take the girls to an indoor play area for about an hour. The truth was that I had to get them out of the house because they were driving me crazy. Chloe had just turned one and was attached to my hip like it was an old, comfortable chair. Mallory was bored with her baby sister, who had little to offer in the way of a playmate.

The entrance price for the play area was six dollars per child per hour. Children under one got in free. You can see where this is going. Yes, I did it. I admit it. I told the cashier that Chloe was under one so that I could get her in free. I figured she just turned one, so I wasn't really ripping anyone off. Plus, I didn't feel like shelling out another six dollars for her to sit on my lap and drool while Mallory played.

"Mommy, Chloe's not eleven months. She's one. Remember we just had her birthday party last week," Mallory said, tugging on the tail of my shirt in a voice loud enough for the cashier and several other mothers to hear.

"Sweetie, we just had her party early, she's not quite one yet," I said, as I imagined the intensity of God's punishing lightning bolt hitting me in the head.

I had sold my soul to the devil for six dollars.

"No, Mommy, for real. You know she's one," Mallory said with pleading eyes and an anxious voice. The cashier was now looking at me pointedly. I think she was also imagining the lightning bolt coming down. "Call Daddy, he'll know," Mallory said, pulling the cell phone from the clip at my belt and handing it to me.

"Mallory, we'll talk about this later," I said between clenched teeth and pulled her into my side.

"But, Mommy!"

The worst part was the smug, knowing expression on the cashier's face. She let Chloe in free, but clearly, she knew I was lying. Worse than that, she knew that I was lying in front of my child and that my child also knew I was lying. I had sold my soul to the devil for six dollars.

So, after a lot of soul-searching and guilt-ridden dreams, I decided to come clean. I sat Mallory down and told her the truth. I felt like the Fonz on *Happy Days*. I had trouble forming the words "I lied, I'm sorry." But they finally came out of my mouth in a rambling, repetitive flow of thoughts that ended with a million mea culpas. She still reminds me of it and probably will for the rest of my life. "Mommy, remember that time you lied about Chloe's age? Try not to do that again, okay?"

"I'll try, honey, I really will," I say, meaning every last word. "But I can't make any promises."

## REALITY MOM

Being a television reporter who covers crime, I see a lot of things most parents don't. I have tried to be honest with my kids about the dangers in the world without going overboard. But sometimes, I go overboard. Okay, I go way overboard. But I bet my six-year-old is the only kid who knows to act like a crazy person if someone tries to abduct her. We've practiced, and let me tell you, it's Oscar-worthy.

I learned this from an article I read years ago where a woman did everything from speak in tongues to throwing up on a guy who tried to rape her. He ultimately left her alone and ran off. The cop was quoted as saying: "There's nothing that scares a criminal more than a crazy person." It made sense to me, and as a result I never forgot it.

If you ask Mallory what happens when you leave your mommy's side in Target, she will tell you that a stranger will take you to heaven and you will never see your parents again. If you ask her what happens when you let go of your mommy's hand in the parking lot, she will promptly tell you that you will be hit by a car and, again, go to heaven.

One day the preschool teacher asked me not to be so *real* with Mallory because she was telling tales to other kids at school. One day my daughter apparently told the kids in her class that two children had been killed in the parking lot of the day care and had gone to heaven. She overheard me talking about two separate news stories where kids had been killed in parking lots, one at a day care (not ours) and one at a fast-food restaurant. Somehow she extrapolated this information and formed her own story. I have to admit, I was kind of impressed, imagining a crowd of wide-eyed children who believed in Santa Claus and the Tooth Fairy gathering around Mallory for the juicy—if fabricated—details, their innocence being sucked from them. In the end, they would be better for it.

It actually made me feel like giving her a little *atta-girl*, but I had to acquiesce to the desires of the teacher. I told Mallory to keep the gory truth just between us.

One day the preschool teacher asked me not to be so *real* with Mallory because she was telling tales to other kids at school.

The one good thing about instilling the proper amount of paranoia in Mallory is that she protects her little sister when they are out and about with their dad and I'm at work. She also tells on him when he doesn't watch Chloe closely.

"Mommy, Daddy just let Chloe run across the parking lot when he was putting stuff in the car at Home Depot, she could have gotten killed. I had to grab her hand," Mallory exclaims emphatically, brushing hair out of eyes full of urgency.

"You did the right thing," I say, giving Grif the evil eye.

"Mommy, Daddy was on the computer. He was ignoring us and Chloe knocked over the lamp and it broke. I had to keep her from getting in the glass," she says, her eyes wide as a deer's in headlights.

"Mommy will take care of it, Sweetheart, go play in your room," I say, picturing shards of glass protruding from my baby's soft white feet.

"Mommy, Daddy left us alone in the car when he went into the dry cleaner. Isn't that against the law?" Mallory says, tugging on my sleeve.

This, of course, does not amuse Grif. He had one female scolding him, now he's got three. It's like he's under a microscope every second of every day. He's actually a very good father, better than most, but like most dads, he's not as aware as most mothers. Clearly, there's a gender component here. Luckily, he's got three women to keep him straight.

. . . . . . . . . . . . . . . . . . . . . . . . . . . . . . . . . . . . . . . . . .

## WASH MY MOUTH OUT

No matter how hard we try, we can't change who we are, even when we become mothers.

There are so many things that come out of my mouth in front of my children that I'm not proud of. I'm constantly assessing the permanent damage that I've already done and estimating how many years it will take to unravel it all.

> When my girls act up in the car, I say, "Do you want Mommy to get a one-way bus ticket to California?"

When my girls act up in the car, I say, "Do you want Mommy to get a one-way bus ticket to California?" This used to make them immediately stop what they were doing and stare straight ahead, contemplating this awful fate. They don't know where California is, or what a one-way ticket is, but they don't like the sound of this option one bit. The problem is now that I've been saying it for so long I think it's losing its effect. Now when I say it they are reduced to fits of laughter in the backseat.

From about eighteen months to about four years old, Mallory was prone to frequent, volatile temper tantrums. I was frustrated. I was exhausted. I won't bore you with the doctors we saw and the medication that we eschewed, but it was rough. In the end we were simply told that she was an emotional child going through a phase and we would have to deal with it. Anyway, during one particularly awful outburst, I asked her if she wanted to go to The Crazy House. I told her that's where kids who lose it like this on a regular basis go.

As soon as it came out of my mouth, I knew it was the wrong thing to say to a young child. I wanted to stuff the words back in. But something came over me at the moment. I was out of control, not physically, but in an emotional and mental sense. All of a sudden I wasn't talking to a child anymore, but to someone who had really pissed me off. I took the low road.

Mallory asked me to describe The Crazy House. This would have been the appropriate time to admit that once again Mommy had fibbed. A sane adult would have turned the train around right there. But I pressed on. The monster was in control. For the first time in a long time I had Mallory's attention. The tantrum had stopped, which in my mind meant the threat worked. So, I continued and made some offhanded remark about straitjackets. That was it. It only happened once—okay, maybe a couple of times. I knew it was so wrong, but it was so effective. She definitely did not like the sound of this place and did not want to go there. Just a mention of The Crazy House was enough to stop a full-throttle temper tantrum dead in its tracks. It was truly magic.

Unfortunately, Mallory told her best friend about The Crazy House. He then told his mother, who of course asked me about it, and that was that. My emotional breakdown, once a personal issue between me and my child, was now out of the bag. No Mother of the Year award for me, no hiding behind my I-can-do-all persona anymore. This time I had to explain myself to an adult.

"Well, you know how you say things you don't really mean in the heat of the moment?" I stammer, not even believing my own words. She smiles a knowing smile and nods. Clearly, she had been in the pit before and, like me, had crawled out, a little muddy, but alive. "It's probably something I need to stop saying . . ."

It was time to have a talk with Mallory. I reluctantly got down on one knee and bared my contrite soul. I told her there was no such thing as a Crazy House for kids. I told her I made the whole thing up to scare her into submission. And once again, I told her I was sorry.

She looks me dead in the eye.

"Another lie?" she says, shaking her head and waving her little finger in my direction. "It's like that time at Party Machine when you lied about Chloe's age. What am I going to do with you, Mommy?"

"I don't know, Sweetie, I really don't know," I say. "Maybe a time-out?"

. . . . . . . . . . . . . . . . . . . . . . . . . . . . . . . . . . . . . . . . .

## POOPING IT UP IN SUBWAY

"Poop number three," Chloe yells from atop the nasty toilet in the bathroom at Subway. She couldn't wait. So now I'm trapped in this bacteria-laden room listening to her count off her humungous poops like a drill sergeant. Inevitably, my Blackberry rings. The caller ID shows me that it's the district attorney. I know I really shouldn't take his call right now, but I also know that he's probably calling me back to give me an update I've been waiting for on an important case.

"Amanda Lamb," I say in the most professional voice I can muster given my surroundings.

"Two more poops to go," Chloe announces as I try to cup my hand around the mouthpiece on my Blackberry to drown out the background noise.

The DA tells me that he's going to take the high-profile assault case to a grand jury on Tuesday and let them decide whether the three defendants should be charged.

"Here comes number four," Chloe screams in the background, completely oblivious to the fact that I'm on the phone, probably because I'm *always* on the phone. Luckily, the DA also doesn't seem to notice that in my world the shit's hitting the fan, literally.

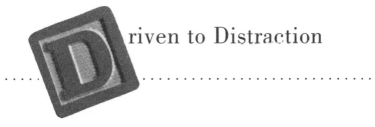

# riven to Distraction

> *"You grow up the day you have the
> first real laugh at yourself."*
> —Ethel Barrymore

When I looked in my rearview window and saw the open newspaper slapping wildly against the windshield of the car behind me, I finally remembered what it was that I had forgotten. I *knew* I'd forgotten *something*. Aha—I'd left the newspaper on the top of the car when I put Chloe in the car seat.

The paper opened in the wind, its pages unfurling and scattering on the hood of the car behind me, completely obstructing the driver's view of the road. How I wished at that moment that I didn't know him—my neighbor.

I've never left a baby on the roof of the car, thank God, but just about everything else has taken a ride there.

One time I was picking up a pizza with both girls with me. Gingerly, I placed the pizza on the roof of the car as I buckled the kids in their car seats. I got into the car, started it up, and had that feeling that I was forgetting something. Realizing my stupidity, I jumped out and grabbed the pizza box off the roof rack. Wow, that was close! Driving down the road delicately so the piping-hot pizza on the front seat would survive the trip, I silently applauded myself for my quick save. I could handle this. I was a pro. Nothing was going to distract me.

When we were about a mile from the pizza place, I heard four-year-old Mallory scream, "Mommy, your wallet!" I looked in my rearview window and saw my black wallet rolling—no, actually, more like bouncing—down the street into traffic. An image flashed through my mind—me standing in line for hours at the DMV to get a new license. That thought alone was enough to prompt me to take quick evasive action.

I did what any Volvo station wagon driver would do: I went off-road, pulled that baby right into the median. I stopped on a dime. I was a woman on a mission. Without hesitation I ran out into traffic, waving my hands wildly in the air. Cars swerved, slamming on brakes. Drivers cursed. I can only imagine what my girls were thinking in the car as they watched their mother's manic display.

Just before a silver minivan was about to decimate my small black wallet with the cute embroidered green "A" on the front, I reached down and scooped it up. I made eye contact with the driver as I held up the wallet triumphantly with both hands like an Olympic medalist. She smiled with a slight nod and raised her hand to let me know she understood. At that moment there was a kinship—just two mothers trying to make it through another day.

## LIFTING THE FOG

I am now in the habit of looking in my rearview mirror every time I leave the driveway. "Oops," I'll say, "there goes my umbrella." Or Mallory will yell, "Mommy, the movie, it fell, they're going to make you buy it again!"

I'm amazed at the ability of some things to hang onto my roof rack. I'll be driving down the road frantically looking for my cell phone. "Mallory," I'll say, "where's Mommy's phone? Have you seen it? Did Mommy have it when I left the house?" Mallory is usually too busy to reply. She's got a head full of car agendas—scribbling in a Barbie coloring book, staring out the window, taking off her sister's socks and shoes. But sometimes she will respond with something like, "Have you looked on top of the car?" I pull to the side of the road and find my little silver mobile phone sitting snugly on the edge of the roof, held there only by the slight rubber edge of the luggage rack and the grace of God. I wonder how it survived. I was going fifty miles an hour and it hung in there. It almost makes me want to experiment with other stuff, nothing really valuable, of course. I think it would be a great *Letterman* segment.

I sometimes wonder how I leave the house with two matching shoes and two children whose shoes also match every day.

Of course, leaving things on the roof of my car is really a symptom of the total cloud of distraction that I live under. I sometimes wonder how I leave the house with two matching shoes and two children whose shoes also match every day. There are some mornings that just the thought of what I must do is so overwhelming I just want to crawl back into bed and fake like I'm sick. But then who would take care of the kids? My live-in maid? No such luck.

I was in Target one day with Chloe and found a cream-colored purse for a family trip we were about to take. I threw it into the cart with the rest of my loot. She immediately reached back into the cart from her perch in the front and started playing with the purse. After selecting a few more items, I headed for the cashier and suddenly noticed the purse was no longer in the cart.

"Chloe, tell Mommy where the purse is," I begged. I frantically circled back to the purse aisle. There was one more left. I checked. Of course it was stained. "Chloe, pleeeeeease tell Mommy where you threw the purse out of the cart so we can go home." Other shoppers looked at me like I was a lunatic talking to a young child this way who clearly couldn't understand what I was asking. But she understood only too well. She fixed her eyes on the floor and refused to answer me.

Finally, I briskly pulled her out of the cart and headed for the door. As I strapped her into the car seat, I explained how the shopping trip had been a complete waste of time and how we would now need to go to another store because she had lost the purse. Just at that moment I felt something hitting me in the side. I reached up and pulled the cream purse off my shoulder. It was confirmed: Not only was I a bad mother but a shoplifter as well.

So I did what any good mother would do. I went back into the store, paid for the purse, and bought my daughter's love back with a lollipop.

## PHONE HOME

The height of my distraction involves the phone. It is my life-line, both for work and for my personal life. People who know me in Raleigh are so used to seeing me with a phone to my ear that they don't even try to have a conversation with me. The parking attendant and the hot dog man silently mouth "Hello" to me as I pass.

It's not uncommon for me to call Grif and then panic. "Oh my God," I say.

"What, what's wrong?" he exclaims.

"I've lost my phone, I can't believe it, I've lost my frigging phone again!"

"Calm down, are you sure? Look around. Is it in your purse, your briefcase? Maybe you left it on your desk at work," he says, having been down this road so many times before he could give tours.

"No, I'm sure this time. I can't find it anywhere. This sucks, I can't believe it, I'm so screwed."

"Amanda," he says in a knowing voice, "if you lost your phone, how are you calling me?"

Slowly, I look to the right. There it is, my little silver phone clasped tightly in my hand.

. . . . . . . . . . . . . . . . . . . . . . . . . . . . . . . . . . . . . . . . . . . . . .

## MOMMY BRAIN

The thing about being a crazy, distracted working mother is that all distractions are not equal. Somehow I can remember that Mallory needs pinecones, a brown sock, and gumdrops for a class project on Thursday. Chloe needs a white sweatshirt, eleven valentines, and a digital picture of herself. I can remember that Lauren, who is having a birthday party on Saturday, is registered at the local toy store and likes ponies. I can remember that Mallory needs tights for ballet, Chloe needs her second flu shot, and there's a prescription for allergy medication waiting at the pharmacy. I have show-and-tell, field trips, playdates, and piano lessons all programmed into my Blackberry. But it's the really common things that I forget. I forget to put on my watch. I forget to bring tampons or an umbrella. I forget where I'm going and drive right past the day care.

"Mommy, you passed our school. Go back! Go back!" Mallory screams at me as she tosses her Barbie coloring book at me.

Luckily she can't remember the times when she was a baby and I passed day care, drove all the way to the office, and realized that she was in the car. But now she knows and is only eager to point out my flaws to her little sister.

I can't wait until they are imperfect parents wading through an ocean of mistakes trying to keep their heads above water.

"Chloe, she did it again, we're going to be late again because Mommy was talking on the phone," Mallory says, her arms crossed and her little lips pursed. Chloe on cue then assumes the same position. I look at their puss faces in the rearview mirror and shake my head. I've disappointed them yet again. I can't wait until they are imperfect parents wading through an ocean of mistakes trying to keep their heads above water. I only hope I live long enough to see it.

# able for One

When I was a child, I did not allow the items on my plate to touch. God forbid the juice from my green beans might snake across the white porcelain dish and attack my mashed potatoes, rendering them inedible. At the beginning of the meal, I would carefully separate my meat, potatoes, and vegetables with invisible walls, making sure there was a sufficient distance to keep them from mingling. If contamination did occur, it was all over. To this day, at salad bars I still must use partitioned plates for the very same reason. I'm not the fanatic I once was, but you know what they say, once obsessive-compulsive, always obsessive-compulsive.

This eating defect has mutated in my oldest child and become even more complex. Mallory won't allow her fork to be polluted by different foods. She needs a separate fork for each item on her plate. This creates a situation where we have to run our dishwasher quite frequently. It's also an issue in restaurants when we have to ask for multiple forks along with every meal.

At home I've resorted to plastic forks to keep from having to run the dishwasher every five minutes. Landfills be damned.

"Yeah, we'll take the chicken nuggets, fries, and side of fruit for her, and three forks, please," I say, trying not to make eye contact with the waitress, knowing that she will barely remember our order, let alone this oddball request.

As expected, the meal comes and we have to ask for more utensils. I consider serving her only finger food for the rest of her life.

· · · · · · · · · · · · · · · · · · · · · · · · · · · · · · · · · · ·

## GAG ME

In addition to making me cut the crusts off her bread and other very specific dietary requests, Mallory has inherited my limited palate. Basically, she likes nothing. She adheres strictly to three food groups—pizza, chicken nuggets, and sweets. I've tried to model better eating habits in front of her, eating more fruits and salads, and I frequently cook things for her that I don't like in an effort to get her to eat a more balanced diet. But, like every other exposed parental flaw, this one is in my blood and is genetically reproduced in my daughter.

As a child I ate only white food—pears, potatoes, cheese, pasta, and bread. It was a control issue, according to articles I've seen in *Parenting* magazine. But in the late '60s, early '70s, we had no such convenient phrases or psychological diagnoses to wrap our children's bizarre behavior up in a box with a neat bow. Basically, kids who didn't conform to the norm were nuts.

My parents were so alarmed by the thought I might starve to death that they took me to a behavioral psychologist. He asked me to draw pictures and observed me playing. Then he asked me what I liked to eat. A skilled manipulator from a young age, I lied and it worked. He told my parents I was fine.

I told him I like everything, including broccoli, peas, and asparagus. He tested me by offering me single bites of food that I refused to eat at home. Every time I would eat a bite of something I didn't like, he would give me an M&M. Voila! I was cured! To this day I eat M&Ms only one at a time.

**I figure anyone who eats boogers on a regular basis can't be that picky.**

My parents adopted a process at home by which I would get a star on a calendar every time I ate my dinner. If I got five in a week, my father would bring me a prize on Friday. The first week I got five stars he brought me bubble gum and baseball cards. It looked like a win-win situation for me, so I kept it up. The second week I made five stars he brought me a small laundry basket so I could be "just like Mommy," doing chores around the house. That was it. I was over that stupid

game. Even when I was four years old, laundry looked like a bitch to me. I refused to eat anything but white food for the next fourteen years.

Luckily, Chloe, who is round and happy, has inherited her father's appetite. She likes to eat everything from boogers to steak and is more willing than her sister to try new foods. I figure anyone who eats boogers on a regular basis can't be that picky. In fact she likes them so much that she's renamed her favorite restaurant "Booger King."

"Chloe, what are you eating, Sweetie?" I ask, dreading the answer.

"Boogers," she says matter-of-factly, pausing her chewing motion for just a split second to answer my question.

"Sweetie, boogers are dirty, you really shouldn't eat them," I say, feeling sick to my stomach.

"I don't care, I like them," she smiles. It makes me think about all of the things I've eaten in my life that I know are bad for me, but I just don't care—cookie dough straight from the freezer, deep-fried cheese, bacon dripping with fat and nitrates. I guess boogers aren't really all that bad after all.

## DOG DAYS

When your child eats *anything*, it can be a blessing and a curse. I learned this the day Chloe became a dog.

"Get that leash off your little sister, Mallory, she's going to choke," I screamed as I watched Chloe being led around the kitchen on all fours.

"But I'm a dog," her little voice chirped from beneath the kitchen table where I had been working. She was looking for crumbs just like our dogs Max and Maggie, who Grif forgets to feed. When I ask him about his lack of consideration, he tells me he has them on a diet. I use the dogs to clean up things like rice and other stray bits of food that end up on the floor after a meal. It's convenient.

The girls love Max and Maggie. So I put up with their poop piles by my front door, their barking that sends neighbors to my door with angry protests, and their smell (not unlike feeding them, Grif is not big on grooming them).

But I draw the line at my child learning to eat off the floor like a dog.

I shoo Chloe away from the crumbs beneath the table. A few minutes later I hear a crunching noise coming from the pantry where Maggie usually eats and sleeps. The problem is that Maggie is outside.

"Chloe, honey, is that you? What are you doing?" I say, knowing full well what she is up to.

"Eating," she says in the muffled tone of someone with a full mouth.

"Eating what, sweetheart?" I ask.

"Dog food, Mommy, remember. I'm a dog."

. . . . . . . . . . . . . . . . . . . . . . . . . . . . . . . . . . . . . . .

## SPICY CHICKEN BITS

When your child finally goes to school, you're secretly thrilled that at least one meal a day is taken care of—lunch. I allowed Mallory to bring her lunch for the first few weeks, and then I started lobbying for the school menu on a daily basis.

"How about spicy chicken bits and corn, wow, that sounds great! I bet you're going to want to buy lunch tomorrow, huh?"

"No, I think I'd rather you make me lunch."

I realized I was going to have to get more creative fast.

"Wow, I can't believe this, spicy chicken tenders on a roll with creamed corn—doesn't that sound absolutely delicious," I say, looking at her hopefully. "I bet that would go well with chocolate milk."

"Well, the chocolate milk does sound pretty good. Maybe I'll bring my lunch, but buy chocolate milk," she says with delight.

My heart sank. I am doomed to getting up early enough to make a turkey sandwich without crusts every frigging morning.

"Okay, I think we got it today, Mallory," I say. "Spicy chicken pieces and corn on the cob. But here's the kicker, the dessert is blueberry cobbler." I lick my lips for emphasis.

"Well, okay," she says. "I guess I could try buying lunch."

After that, she actually wanted to buy lunch as long as there was something involving spicy chicken parts on the menu— nuggets, bits, pieces, tenders. Any variation of the theme would do. If I forgot to look at the menu and sent her to school with a packed lunch on a chicken bit day, I had hell to pay.

"Mommy, I'm so mad at you. It was a spicy chicken burger on a roll today," she says, handing me her lunch box with the un- eaten turkey sandwich inside. "Why did you send my lunch?"

Clearly, it all worked out okay. She had purchased the spicy chicken burger on a roll instead of eating her soggy turkey sandwich. But I guess it was the mere inconvenience of having to lug the full Hello Kitty lunch box back and forth to school that made her mad.

I still make her lunch on spaghetti day (the sauce is too sweet), turkey fryer day (what is that anyway?), and corn dog day (just plain gross). We're both scared of cheese dipper day, but that usually falls on Friday when I'm off; I bring McDonald's for both of us and join her in the cafeteria.

I don't mind making lunch occasionally. I just wish I didn't have to deal with the whole tedious crust-cutting-off thing. The other day I finally asked her how long I would have to continue cutting the crusts off her bread.

"After the first week in second grade," she answered definitively.

At least I don't have to guess.

## PASS THE FOIE GRAS, PLEASE

One absolute is that children cannot eat late. The later you begin the adventure, the more problems you are asking for. My parents, however, still don't get this. Sometimes it amazes me that they raised children of their own. It's as if all the wisdom and experience they gleaned from parenting evaporates with every passing year and every glass of scotch.

"Dad," I'll say when we go on vacation with my father and his wife, "we really need to eat early with the kids."

"Okay, sure, sure, like seven?" he says.

"I was thinking more like 5:30. They're going to be really tired after being at the beach all day," I say, knowing he won't bite. Again, same conversation, different day.

"That's too early. Seven will be good," he says, taking another sip of his scotch.

"Well, maybe we should just get a sitter, or Grif will stay with the kids. I know they're going to act up. We'll all be miserable," I plead.

"Let's try it, they'll be fine." Stated like a man who has never seen my kids go ballistic in a restaurant before. Of course, he *has* seen this many times and is always incredulous. The scotch has clearly put a dent in his long-term memory.

He always took us to the same little hole-in-the-wall Italian restaurant in Wildwood, New Jersey. It's a place where you can get a big slice of pizza and a little slice of Mafia, or at least that's what my dad thinks—he's a WASP who has watched way too many episodes of *The Sopranos*. My dad and my stepmother enjoy good food, so for them coming here is really slumming it. I'm used to eating the number-six meal from McDonald's at eighty miles an hour in the passenger seat of a news car, so for me, any restaurant with cloth napkins is a treat.

It's a place where you can bring kids, but the question is: *Should* you bring kids? Grif jokes that he heard the food is great but he has never eaten a meal there in six years because he is always forced to leave with one or both of our screaming children before the order arrives.

Last year's dinner was the worst. After a long day on the water, we showered the girls and dressed them in cute matching outfits. The theory is that the cuter they are, the less likely they will annoy people.

"Oh, honey," a nearby diner might say, "see that adorable child eating spaghetti with her hands, isn't she just wearing the cutest dress?"

My cousin brought her five-year-old daughter, Lily, who was a companion for Mallory and a welcome distraction from bad behavior. Lily is an only child and is used to eating with adults. She modeled appropriate table behavior that kept Mallory in check for the most part. At the same time Lily is a constant, painful reminder that I have *spirited* children.

Chloe, on the other hand, was exhausted. She promptly crawled into my lap as if preparing to sleep for the night. My father ran out to his car and got a towel to cover her with so that she wouldn't be cold due to the air-conditioning blasting on us from the ceiling. It was one of his dog's towels, but he assured me it had been washed. Unlike me, my dad is a dog person. It's just one more thing that we disagree about, especially when he tries to compare his standard poodle's developmental milestones to Chloe's. He and his wife claim to be dog rescuers. I keep waiting for them to rescue my dogs. If any dogs need rescuing, it's mine.

Anyway, as I sat there swishing a nice glass of Cabernet, I thought how amazing it was to finally be eating a meal with my family on vacation where my kids were not melting down.

Suddenly, Chloe sat up and looked groggily around the restaurant. She looked as if she were going to cry. Clearly, she didn't know where she was. So I rubbed her back and spoke some soothing words to her in a quiet voice about getting her a glass of milk. Then it happened. The unthinkable. She pulled a Linda Blair straight out of *The Exorcist.* Projectile vomit started spewing out of her mouth in multiple directions. Grif sprang into action, using the towel to shield others from the blast of yellow goo cascading out of my beautiful little girl's mouth. No cute dress could counteract this one. I knew we would never make it to the bathroom without spraying at least five tables, so I did what any mother would do. I encouraged her to get it all out and told her it would be okay.

> This was it, the last straw, the final attempt for my children to coexist with my old-money family.

"Don't worry, Sweetie, Mommy's here," I said, trying not to sound alarmed. "It's going to be okay, just get it all out. Don't be scared, it's okay."

But I knew it would not be okay. It would never be okay for me to take my children to a restaurant with my parents again. This was it, the last straw, the final attempt for my children to coexist with my old-money family who preferred foie gras to chicken nuggets and rarely went to restaurants that allowed patrons to wear jeans, even designer jeans.

I can still see my stepmother's face in slow motion as she held her hand over her martini glass to protect it from the flying vomit. You have to understand. This martini was hard fought for. It takes more time for her to order it than it does for her to drink it. I can't remember the specifics, but I know shards of ice are part of the recipe—not chunks, dear God.

Grif whisked Chloe out of the restaurant, mumbling apologies. The waitress assured me it was fine, there was nothing to be embarrassed about, children get sick. Yet my family acted as if they had just seen someone beheaded with a sickle.

# Holidays on Xanax

*"It's better to die on your feet than to
live on your knees."*
—Delores Ibarruri

No one told me you had to put vinegar in the water with the little tablets. Seriously, who knows that? Well, apparently the rest
of the world does because I'm the only idiot whose Easter eggs
come out looking sickly and pale instead of like the bright, colorful ones on the box.

"Why are you even doing that?" Grif asks. I balance Chloe
on my knee and guide her small hand carefully over the cup.
She is precariously balancing an egg on the edge of the little
bent wire spoon that comes in the box. It hangs just above a full
cup of purple dye. One wrong move and the dye splashes all
over me and the carpet.

"I'm doing it because it's Easter, silly. Kids love dyeing
eggs," I say. "I did it with my mom, didn't you?" Mallory pulls
her egg out of the orange dye and examines it for any trace of
color. There is no color at all because I forgot the stupid vinegar.

"No, actually we never did that," Grif says. His upbringing
was not Norman Rockwell-esque. While he was loved, sometimes

things were missing—like living room furniture, a paved driveway, and traditions like dyeing Easter eggs.

"Well, then you probably can't help me. I'm just frustrated because these eggs don't seem to be holding the color. I can't figure it out," I say, bewildered. I have a master's degree in journalism from a prestigious university, but no common sense.

"Well, for starters you might try using white eggs instead of brown eggs," Grif says, walking out of the room.

## EASTER GEEK

Just like everything else we do with children these days, holidays are overdone—and too long. Easter, rather than being a day, is weeks of Easter egg hunts—and that annoying plastic grass. Plastic grass stuck to my ass is another indication that I'm no longer cool.

What I hate more than plastic grass is the competitive drive for eggs. At church, at family gatherings, at friends' parties—it doesn't matter, it's a free-for-all. Mallory, the competitive little devil that she is, races to take every egg she can right out from under the noses of small, unsuspecting toddlers. Chloe cries about thirty seconds into the event because she can't find any eggs and her sister won't help her. I sneak several eggs out of Mallory's basket (which is usually about to fall over because it's so top-heavy) and then drop them at Chloe's feet so she can *find* them.

I'm pretty lame at dressing the girls in Easter outfits. I think this goes back to when I was about four and my mother made me wear a big, white straw Easter hat with a massive bow. The hat might have been cute except that I had on white gloves, wire-framed glasses, and a big, blue wool coat with bright gold buttons—and I was holding a stuffed skunk, of all things. The real beauty of this image is that I don't actually remember it; I just have a photo of myself—the Easter geek in all her glory.

So with my girls I try, I really do try, to make them look cute at Easter. Cute, but not matching. I try to put them in complementary outfits so that when you take their picture they look like the kids who came with the frame. I even pull out the bows for the occasion. I brush and I brush, and I twist their little strands of hair until I can figure out where the bows might actually stay put. In short, I pretend like I know what I'm doing.

"Mommy, that doesn't look right," Mallory says, eyeing herself in the mirror with a cockeyed blue bow barely hanging onto the side of her head. It actually looks more like some kind of an unnatural growth than a hair adornment. "It's not the way Aunt Jennifer does it."

"I'm trying, okay?" I say, poised with the brush above her little head. I tug harder on the strands, trying to get them to stay in one place so I can grab a little clump of it. I can barely put my own hair in a ponytail let alone put a complicated bow in someone else's hair.

"Maybe we should just forget about the bow," Mallory says, frowning. She's onto me again. She can see through my faux attempt at hairstyling confidence.

"No, we'll get it, you'll see," I say, feeling my palms sweat as I try to force the clip attached to the bow around a thick wad of hair.

"Maybe you should call Aunt Jennifer and ask her how she does it," Mallory suggests.

"Maybe you should remember who dyed two dozen Easter eggs with you," I reply.

"But they have no color, Mommy, no color. It's not the way they look on the box, is it?" She pulls the bow out of my other hand and tries to put it in herself.

"No, they don't, Baby, no, they don't. But they're *our* stinking eggs. Who cares if they're not all that bright? They're subtle. Subtle is good. Subtle eggs, subtle hair. You don't need the silly bow," I say, taking her hand. "You look great just the way you are."

"I think you're right, Mommy," she says, smoothing her hair.

"I *know* I'm right," I say, looking at the beautiful little girl in the mirror smiling back at me.

· · · · · · · · · · · · · · · · · · · · · · · · · · · · · · · · · · · · · ·

## DON'T BE MY VALENTINE

There are many things in life that take on new magic when you have children because you are experiencing the joy through their eyes. For me this includes simple things like the first time a child dips her feet into a wave as the white foam curls around her little toes, or the first time she sees big, white fluffy snowflakes falling from the sky. But for me, Valentine's Day isn't one of those magical moments that make motherhood worthwhile.

Day-care and school teachers send home notes telling parents to make sure they write and label valentines for everyone in the class. We have become a society that values inclusion above everything else. I totally get this. It's a noble venture. But mommies must sign and address all the teeny-tiny valentines, not to mention fold them just right, seal them, and somehow attach a piece of candy if you don't want to be outdone by other mothers, good mothers, better mothers. The process is not only tedious, it's ludicrous. I never received valentines before I was old enough to write, why should my kids?

After about age five, in my opinion, it's up to the kid. I buy them, and Mallory signs and addresses them. If she misses someone, oh well. It's not my problem if little David gets his heart broken because she forgot to give him a Hello Kitty valentine with a lollipop taped so securely to the envelope that he would have needed a blowtorch to get it off.

Last year I got the cheapest box of valentines I could find for Chloe's class. They all contained characters from a Disney movie and featured cute sayings like "You're a princess; you deserve royal treatment on Valentine's Day." It wasn't until I was on the eighteenth valentine that I realized every card had a princess theme and about half of Chloe's class is male. Another mother would have thrown them away and gotten new ones for the boys. Not me. Those boys would just have to deal with being little princesses for a day.

Mallory and Chloe come home with brown paper bags overflowing with the same little cheap valentines that they handed out to their classmates. My favorite cards are the ones where the mothers use the fake kid signature. You know, where you use your non-writing hand and labor to make each letter so it looks like your kid signed it? I admit, sometimes when I'm in a real hurry I still do this on thank-you notes. Someone sitting next to me on a plane busted me doing this on long-overdue thank-you notes. I really didn't care because I didn't know the man, and he wasn't likely to get a thank-you note from Mallory's sixth birthday party.

Just getting a valentine from anyone other than my kids or my husband annoys me, because then I have to think about mailing one in return. But I've learned to chuck both the card and the guilt.

"My Mommy isn't funny, but she is smart."

There's only one kind of valentine that actually makes me a little misty-eyed: the ones addressed to "Mommy." Mallory made one for me that said, "My Mommy isn't funny, but she is smart."

You're not going to find that one at a Hallmark store. I guarantee it.

. . . . . . . . . . . . . . . . . . . . . . . . . . . . . . . . . . . . . . . . . . . . . .

## COWGIRL

Halloween has always been one of my favorite holidays, mostly because I love to dress up and look cute. I think it taps into my inner hidden desire to have been an actress. I did act in high school, but I never got the lead in the school play, and I certainly never got the chance to look cute on stage. So, for Halloween, I've always chosen outfits that make me look sexy: You know—hookers and rock stars. But now that I have kids, Halloween isn't for *me* anymore, it's for them.

Not unlike Easter, there is an endless stream of parties during the Halloween "season." Because Mallory is allergic to nuts, I have the added stress of having to be at every party and monitor her candy intake and examine every bag of candy that comes home from every party. The good news is that *I'm* not allergic to nuts, so I usually make out pretty well with Mallory's leftovers. I hoard Reese's cups in a special hiding place so that I can binge on them when I've had a particularly hard day.

For most little girls Halloween is all about being a princess. There are many variations of princesses. There are Disney princesses like Ariel and Belle. And there are just good, old-fashioned princesses with big, pink, puffy dresses and jeweled crowns. But not my kid—no way, last year Mallory wanted to be a cow.

"You know cows are fat, right?" I say as I try logic on her five-year-old brain. "And they're farm animals, smelly farm animals." I hold my nose for effect. It's not like I'm ready for her to be a hooker or a rock star, I just can't figure out why she won't be a frigging princess like every other little girl on our street. I've got a million princess costumes in our dress-up box that I could dry-clean and, voila, instant Halloween costume.

"I don't care. I want to be a cow," she says, pointing to a cow costume in a magazine. The costume comes in sizes six months to eighteen months, because little girls generally don't want to be cows for Halloween.

"You sure you don't want to be a princess or a cheerleader?" I ask. "We have lots of that stuff in the dress-up box." I smile anxiously, realizing I would have to *make* a costume, something I hoped I would never have to do. I can barely thread a needle, let alone sew something from scratch. I remember when I was growing up, some mothers made things from patterns. One time I asked my mother about patterns and why she never used them. They seemed like some mysterious treasure maps and for some reason our family didn't possess any. She told me it was nothing a smart girl like me needed to worry about. So here I am, forty, and I can barely sew a button on a blouse. How's that for smart?

I figured if I couldn't make the cow costume, surely I could buy it. I quickly discovered that the problem with cow costumes is that they come in two sizes—adult and baby. So I had to buck up and face the task at hand. How hard could this be?

We spent one Saturday afternoon driving around to every costume shop and craft store in town looking for things to make the cow outfit. I ended up buying a fake cat's tail and a bell meant for a birdcage. I fashioned a cow's tail from the cat's tail. I hung the square bell around her neck and used black paint to create ears and athletic socks to make hooves. To top off the look, I borrowed a cow-patterned vest. In the end, my little cow was quite cute. Her cow was much cuter than my hooker.

> Her cow was much cuter than my hooker.

I had borrowed a caterpillar suit for Chloe. She found it in her closet about two weeks before Halloween and decided she needed to wear it every day up until we went trick-or-treating. I would hear the *swish, swish, swish* of the caterpillar tail dragging down the hallway across the carpet.

"Chloe, is that you?" I'd say, looking up from my computer.

"Yes, Mommy, it's just me, the caterpillar," she'd say, proudly mastering the new word.

"Don't mess it up, you have to wear that on Halloween," I'd say for the twentieth time.

"I won't, Mama, promise," she'd yell. I'd already washed three substances from the costume—jelly, bubble gum, and toothpaste.

When the big day finally comes, a crowd of neighborhood children gathers in the cul-de-sac to make the quarter-mile journey up the street—a plethora of princesses, fairies, and superheroes dressed in fancy Internet-bought or Target-purchased costumes. Just fifteen houses line the street, but there's a lot of loot to be had from upper-middle-class white people who remember the days when we accepted loose candy corns from strangers and didn't worry about anthrax in our candy apples.

The parents are well prepared. The fathers are armed with flashlights and beers. One dad even wears a safety vest. I'm not sure what that's about. But who am I to judge? I'm the one chasing behind my kids, stuffing their Reese's Cups in my mouth.

My little caterpillar and my little cow are surrounded by a sea of glittery girls with sequins, tiaras, and lipstick.

As my little caterpillar and my little cow are surrounded by a sea of glittery girls with sequins, tiaras, and lipstick, I realize just how proud I am to have girls who don't care what everyone else thinks. Unlike Mommy, they will probably not be hookers and rock stars on Halloween when they grow up. And whatever they are, I'm sure they'll always be cute.

## SKIPPING TURKEY DAY

Because I am a television news reporter, I am required to work some holidays. As a senior reporter, though, I get to choose the holidays I want to work. Thanksgiving is a no-brainer. I don't cook. I don't like turkey. I don't watch football. So what's there to like about Thanksgiving?

Grif usually takes the girls to one of his relatives' houses for the holiday. I lay out the cute outfits and bows, kiss them good-bye, and head off to work. I'm glad they have somewhere to go, but I don't miss the festivities for a second. In fact, I'd love to go to London over Thanksgiving weekend, anywhere they don't celebrate this holiday dedicated to outdated ideals of domesticity, gluttony, and television-watching.

In between stories, I eat my Thanksgiving day lunch with a photographer at an all-you-can eat buffet that barely makes a passing sanitation grade. I watch as lonely souls pile turkey and gravy, mashed potatoes, and cranberry sauce a mile high on their plates. We eat elbow-to-elbow at crowded, sticky tables. Waitresses re-fill our water or tea every five minutes, hoping for a big holiday-sympathy tip.

I wonder how all these people got here. Did they leave their wives? Do they have bad blood with their in-laws? Just get out of prison? I'm sure there are a million reasons why they are eating at a nasty buffet and sitting around a crowded table with strangers instead of at home with family.

And the crazy thing is there's no place I'd rather be.

It's in these moments that I just have to bow my head and say a little prayer. It's always the same prayer every year. I tell God that I'm so thankful, thankful that I don't have to cook.

## SAY CHEESE!

Just hearing the word "Christmas" can make my heart skip a beat and my palms sweat. It's not a warm fuzzy feeling. It's a dreaded feeling because I know what I have to do between now and December 25 to make it all come together like Martha Stewart on speed. It starts with the Christmas picture and it ends with a martini and a migraine in the bathtub on Christmas night.

The countdown to Christmas begins in July with the infamous picture that will adorn your Christmas card and travel to dozens of friends all over the world. It may be your only chance to show your family and friends, whom you haven't seen in years, that you did something right—you gave birth to two beautiful people. I mean, isn't that what the Christmas card is really all about? If we really wanted to reach out and touch someone, we'd give her a call. So, it's not really about reconnecting with people you love; it's about showing them you're worth something. We take all those pictures of other people's children and hold them up to ours and say, *we have the cutest kids.*

"Honey, did you see the picture of Max and Ellie's kids, you know, from Utah?" I call from the kitchen into the den.

"Yeah, not so cute?" Grif says with a chuckle.

"No, maybe it's the lighting or the angle," I say, examining the picture under the light.

"Well, Max and Ellie aren't very cute, so it's not totally unexpected," he says as he power-surfs the remote from his deep crevice on the couch.

"True, very true," I say.

The annual responsibilities related to who will take the picture, when we will take it, where we will take it, and what the girls will wear are my domain.

"Where do you think we should take the girls' Christmas picture?" I ask. It's a trick question because I know he doesn't care, but I need to show him that I *do* care.

"Whatever, you pick the place," Grif says absentmindedly, shuffling through mail.

"How about on the train tracks with a train bearing down on them in the background?" I ask, my hands placed squarely on my hips.

"Sounds good, I'm easy," he says, finally looking up from the mail and meeting my glare. "What?"

The Christmas picture experience was easier when it just involved one child. Before Chloe we just dressed Mallory up and let her simply go in front of a camera. One year she was an angel floating on a puffy, white cloud. Another year she was a

Duke cheerleader playing in a pile of leaves. After taking about seventy-five pictures, there was always *one*. All you need is *one good shot*.

But then there were two. Getting two children to look equally as cute *and* look at the camera is more than a challenge—it's almost a mathematical impossibility.

I am very fortunate to have a sister-in-law, Jennifer, who is an excellent photographer. *She* is now in charge of my Christmas picture and hence has become a partner in choosing the location and the outfits. Last year we picked the outside of my church, which was built in the mid-1800s and has more character than my Great Aunt Wilhelmina.

> Getting two children to look equally as cute *and* look at the camera is more than a challenge—it's almost a mathematical impossibility.

We had a small window of light in front of the church, as well as a small window of time before the 5:00 p.m. service to get the perfect holiday picture. The first five minutes went well. They tilted their little heads, made half-smiles, and acted like they actually liked one another. But then things deteriorated quickly. Chloe refused to take her hand out of her mouth. Then like a spoiled child actor she refused to pose without a bribe of crackers just out of frame. Finally, she refused to cooperate at all.

In the end we got *one* good picture, which of course is all you really need.

## PINE-SCENTED AIR FRESHENER

As a child I remember decorating the Christmas tree with my mother—sharing laughter and a cup of eggnog, Christmas carols playing in the background. Fast-forward thirty years. My mother now has her maid decorate her Christmas tree because she is too busy. I begrudgingly decorate our tree after Grif begrudgingly hauls it down from the attic and puts it together. I spray it with evergreen air freshener (my mother's idea) so that it smells real. My girls think it's a holiday tradition to match the colored tape on the end of the branches into the corresponding notches on the tree trunk.

Growing up, we always had fake trees and I never felt like I missed out because of it. Catherine Crimsler was the one of the few people I knew who had a real tree. It was so tall it almost touched the ceiling in her parents' two-story foyer. There was no way anyone could decorate it without a ladder and maybe a crane. And the aroma was overwhelming. It made the whole house smell like Christmas for the entire month of December. But Catherine Crimsler's daddy drank too much and her mommy was always crying loudly behind a locked door in the bathroom, so I figured a real tree didn't make people all that happy.

There's that thrilling moment when Grif makes one final grunt and shoves the tree box through the slender opening in our pull-down attic so that it crashes onto the floor below. This is usually followed by him yelling down to me, "Do we really need to put up all this shit?"

We skip eggnog and go right to hard liquor. Then Grif begins the decorating process by untangling twenty-seven strands of lights. After painstakingly laying them out, connecting them, and then delicately wrapping them around the tree, there is always, I mean *always*, a strand that doesn't work. The girls sit at his feet and watch the scene unfold with glee. It's like something out of those bad G-rated holiday movies when the bumbling dad just can't get anything right. Grif runs to the store to get more lights, which grinds the decorating process to a halt, because you can't put the balls on before the lights. I urge him to take the kids to the store with him so I can lie on the couch and drink more while I hum along with my cheesy holiday CD.

> We skip eggnog and go right to hard liquor. Then Grif begins the decorating process by untangling twenty-seven strands of lights.

When he finally returns from the store and gets the lights right, it's my turn. Unlike some sentimental people who save all of their children's handcrafted ornaments and adorn their tree with them, I have what some people would call a designer tree. I only allow red, gold, and glass balls evenly spaced throughout the tree. Not only is this not a fun decorating experience with children, it's *painful*. We lose a lot of balls along the way because little hands can't always hold them securely or put them in the awkward places that I want them.

"Okay, Sweetie, if you stand on your tiptoes you can get it on that branch," I direct Mallory. "No, a little to the left, a little more, we can't have two red balls too close together, can we?"

The experience also prompts them to wonder aloud where their homemade ornaments have gone—ornaments that I can't believe they remember an entire year later.

"Mommy, where is the squishy snowball thing with the glitter and the ribbons that I made at Lindsey's party?" Mallory asks as she takes yet another gold ball out of the box.

"Gee, honey, we'll have to look for that," I say.

But in the end, we all stand around the perfectly coiffed tree admiring the spacing of the balls we didn't break, thinking, *damn, we did a good job!* We ignore the holes where we somehow lost a branch between the attic and the den. We drink in the smell of the evergreen air freshener and we think, *what could make this more perfect?*

There's only one thing—a tree with built-in lights.

. . . . . . . . . . . . . . . . . . . . . . . . . . . . . . . . . . . . . . . .

## DON'T CREASE THE NAPKINS

The holiday dinner is the culmination of weeks of planning and general chaos that begins Thanksgiving weekend. And this is my mother's domain.

For several years she ironed my napkins. She ironed them late on Christmas Eve, after we returned from church. It was almost too much for me to bear watching her. Ironing napkins is like polishing silver; it's just not something I'm going to do in my lifetime. Why iron when you can dry-clean? Why polish silver when you can just run it through the dishwasher and hope for the best?

"Mother, everyone who is coming is either crazy or will be sauced, so why do the napkins have to be perfect?" I ask. I mean it. Between odd family members and odd friends, we have a motley crew at our holiday table. Fueled by alcohol, emotional instability, and perceived injustices done to one another, there is always drama—and rarely does it center on wrinkled napkins.

There will always be melodrama served at my Christmas table, but you won't find a creased napkin.

"They just do," she says with the haggard look of a Depression-era housewife trying to keep up a good front for the family even though they're down to cornmeal and pocket change.

And so I now have the napkins dry-cleaned. This satisfies my mother's perverse need to have a perfect Christmas table and frees me of the guilt of watching her press the linens into submission. There will always be melodrama served at my Christmas table, but you won't find a creased napkin.

## SANTA STUCK IN THE CHIMNEY

Mallory is on to all of these fake Santas who sit pompously in their red velvet chairs, holding court at the mall or at my company Christmas party.

"Mommy, that Santa has sneakers on and his beard is definitely not real," she says, pointing to the Santa Claus outside Nordstrom's.

"Well, maybe he was really busy and needed to wear sneakers so he could get around fast," I reply. "And maybe he cut his beard off and regretted it, so he is wearing a fake one until the real one grows back."

"No, that's not it," Mallory says, shaking her head and tightening her grip on my hand as we close in on the imposter. "He's just a fill-in Santa. There are a lot of them. Probably as many as there are elves." She looks up at me with her big brown eyes.

"Interesting, why do you think that is?" I say, amazed at the wheels I can almost see turning in her little head.

"I bet it's because the real Santa got stuck in a chimney and he had to call 9-1-1 on his cell phone to get help," she says. "He's pretty fat, you know, and chimneys—well, chimneys are really tight!"

# arty Girls

*"There is no pleasure in having nothing to do; the fun is having lots to do and not doing it."*
—Mary Wilson Little

There's nothing more uncomfortable than watching a bad comedian. It's like being awake during a colonoscopy. It's almost too painful to watch.

But put a bad comedian in a room full of children, and he'll think he's died and gone to *Saturday Night Live*. Kids laugh at absolutely everything. Think about it; they laugh at potty words. When's the last time the word "poop" sent you into fits of laughter? They laugh at anything punctuated by the word "booger." Mommy-booger, Daddy-booger, Mallory-booger . . . you get the idea.

I attended Amy's pirate party for her six-year-old son, and naturally she hired a pirate to entertain the kids with pirate magic tricks, whatever those are. Because the party happened to fall on the same day as the biggest arts and crafts festival in our town, most of the really good pirates were taken. Let's just say she got a B-team pirate at best.

First of all, the guy was pushing seventy and looked nothing like a pirate despite his get-up. He had glasses; a small, scraggly moustache; a drawn, wrinkled face; and just a tuft of hair. He pretended to drink rum throughout the entire routine, yelling *aargh* after each gulp. Toward the end of his act, I started to think he might have the real thing in his little flask.

Then he did something really scary. He took out a guillotine—yes, a *guillotine*—to cut stuff up in front of an audience of little kids. At this point my concern about the pretend rum in the flask grew. Obviously, drinking and operating a guillotine isn't a good combination. He even made one little boy shrink away in shame because the kid refused to put his arm in the contraption. I was shocked that he shamed a child—I thought only clowns did that.

The craziest thing was the kids laughed their heads off. They literally guffawed, throwing themselves head first from their little crossed-leg positions onto the carpet in front of them. They screamed for more like a drug-crazed crowd at a rock concert. I started wondering if the pirate had passed the flask around the room. The more the kids laughed, the longer he performed. He was in his heyday. He had never had an audience like this before, at least not since the late '70s, and, by God, he was going to milk it for everything it was worth.

"I only paid him for half an hour. Why is he still going?" Amy asked me from where she sat on the floor in a sea of hysterical children. "Who does that?"

"Isn't it obvious?" I said. "He's playing to a packed house and getting great reviews, there's no stopping him. He'll be here all night. You'll never get rid of him."

. . . . . . . . . . . . . . . . . . . . . . . . . . . . . . . . . . . . .

## COIN TOSS

I'll trade you a Chuck E. Cheese for two Bullwinkle's and a Tumblebus," I say, wondering if Grif is naïve enough to take the bait. I wring my hands and wait patiently for his answer.

"I'll see your Bullwinkle's and Tumblebus and even throw in a Pump It Up if you take two Jellybeans," he says with a grin, thinking he's trumped my offer.

These negotiations are about our daughters' social schedule. Like Paris and Nikki Hilton, our girls are invited to multiple parties every weekend. It is an endless stream of loud, crowded kid places, cold pizza, and store-bought birthday cake.

Our mothers simply pulled out the pin the tail on the donkey, dusted off party hats from last year, made a Betty Crocker cake, and called it a day. The funny thing is, I don't remember thinking this was a bad way to have a birthday party. In fact, at the time, I'm sure I thought it was pretty cool. Because my birthday is in June, we always had backyard pool parties, which all kids love. Back then nobody worried about liability—they just let us swim. There were no floaties, life jackets, or other safety devices designed to keep our heads above water. It was sink or swim. Somehow, most of us learned to swim and lived to tell the story.

But birthday parties at home have pretty much become a thing of the past. With the exception of my friend Amy, I don't know anyone who hosts birthday parties at home anymore. It's simply unheard of, and when it does happen, other moms are surprised by the courage of the mother throwing the party.

"Ann's party is at her *house?*" I ask Mallory. "I mean, how is her mother going to entertain the kids?"

The truth is we don't have parties at home anymore because we don't want little brats running around destroying our houses. Plus, kids today have such high expectations of being constantly entertained, few mothers have the talent or stamina to feed their bottomless little pits of need.

I wish I had come up with some of these places they have today where you can host children's birthday parties. I mean, a hollowed-out bus where kids roll around? Blow-up slides in a big warehouse? A miniature gym for Lilliputians? A dancing, singing, larger-than-life mouse? It's like those mothers who have a simple idea and then make a million dollars. I bet the disposable-bib lady is laughing all the way to the bank.

> Plus, kids today have such high expectations of being constantly entertained, few mothers have the talent or stamina to feed their bottomless little pits of need.

The problem with the birthday party venues is that they are very public and very crowded. I can't drop my daughters off; every pedophile on the North Carolina Sex Offender registry probably goes to the roller rink. has chosen this day to go roller-skating. So I have to stay and suffer through the mind-numbing chaos. I mean, I would seriously rather lose a limb than dart up into the climbing structure at Bullwinkle's one more time to save a stranded child. Believe me, it's happened with both girls on more than on occasion. This is no McDonald's Playland, mind you. This is a gargantuan structure with twists and turns worthy of a professional mountain climber.

You need a map and a compass to get back to your mother.

I can see it about to happen. Chloe gets trapped on level four. Her little face is peering down at me through the black netting. Suddenly, three kids smash her into the corner of the platform she is standing on. Then there is the birdlike screech that could only be coming from my baby.

"Mama, help, I need you!" she blurts, somehow audible over the din of the video games and cheesy music.

Like a pro, I rip off my shoes (because it's against the rules to wear shoes in the climbing structure) and prepare for my search-and-rescue mission. I quickly survey the situation and realize that climbing up the slide is going to be my fastest route. (This too is against the rules, but I ignore this minor detail in favor of efficiency.) I get a running start and bolt up the yellow slide, narrowly missing a child coming down.

By now Chloe's screeching has become a cacophony of guttural noises that should not be coming from a small child, especially a really cute one. I can feel the eyes of the crowd on my back. I muscle my way through packs of boys on my way up and crawl through the tunnel, scraping my knees on the hard plastic. I'm determined; I feel no pain.

When I finally arrive at level four, I pull Chloe tightly to my chest. *I am here. Mommy is here. Everything is going to be all right,* I say with my hug. There is no need for words. She holds me for a minute and then pulls away. She grins.

"Hi, Mama. Want to go down the slide with me?"

## ROLLING WITH IT

I chaperone the girls to roller-skating parties because I know how to roller-skate and Grif does not.

I could have fast-forwarded my life and predicted this, but I didn't, just like Grif didn't see the old man in the velour track suit that day in 1995 on the boardwalk in Venice Beach, California.

We were visiting friends and decided to rent in-line skates and cruise along the boardwalk. Not to be outdone by his new, sexy, Rollerblading girlfriend, Grif told me he wasn't a great skater but that he could handle it. I think it was about seven minutes into the skate when he collided with the old man on a bike. They ended a twisted pile of metal and velour in the middle of the boardwalk. I saw it coming, but there was nothing I could do to prevent it. So, I decided to jump out of the way into the sand and not add myself to the pile. Hence, I'm now in charge of all roller-skating birthday parties.

**Radnor Rolls is where I first learned to French kiss—yet another reason I will never leave my girls unattended at the rink.**

What I hate about roller-skating rinks is that they are loud and dark. What I used to love about roller-skating rinks was that they were loud and dark. In my day I cut a pretty mean figure eight around the rink at Radnor Rolls. With the disco ball cascading dots of light on my tie-dye shirt, my feather earrings and my feathered hair blowing in the breeze created by my speed, I was all-powerful. I was also one of the girls who could backwards skate. This made me a priority pick for the couple's skate. Radnor Rolls is where I first learned to French kiss—yet another reason I will never leave my girls unattended at the rink.

Given that my talent has lain dormant for so many years, it's hard for me not to let loose and strut my stuff and break away to a song like "Dancing Queen."

But it can't happen. Mallory insists that I stay by her side. I can't touch her, mind you. I just hover in case she starts to fall. I'm expected to spring into action and catch her before her little bony butt hits the hardwoods. Mallory doesn't believe that falling is part of learning how to skate. Not my girl, no, she must do everything perfectly or not at all.

Sometimes Mallory lets me skate backwards and hold her hands, pulling her along tentatively. But inevitably this leads to falling. She then nixes the idea in favor of holding onto the wall again. This makes each tour around the rink painfully slow. We could almost *walk* faster; in fact, I'm sure we could walk faster than we're attempting to skate. But for three hours I shuffle alongside her, hoping that at any minute it will simply click for her and she will take off. I want her to feel the breeze in her hair and the thrill of it all.

"Can Mommy just skate around one time without you and come back?" I say, grooving to a Styx tune. "I promise I'll keep my eye on you the entire time."

"Okay, but you have to come right back," she says, keeping her eyes focused straight ahead. She alternately uses her stiff arms to hold onto the side and then to try to let go and glide a little. She shuffles. She is concentrating too hard to be bothered by my obvious need for speed.

For just a moment I am fifteen again, whizzing around the rink, hugging the boards, singing, "Tonight's the night we'll make history, honey you and I!" But as quickly as the dream envelops me, it vanishes. My fantasy is unexpectedly deflated by a little boy who races by and grabs the leg of my jeans as he begins to fall. This starts a chain reaction, and suddenly I am in the middle of a pile of whining children. My underwear is sticking out of my low-rise jeans. I awkwardly try to pull my pants up with one hand as I attempt to detangle myself from the pack.

"You're not really that good, Mommy, are you?" Mallory says when I return to her side.

"No, not anymore, Baby, but I *was*, believe me, I was," I say, picturing the girl under the disco ball who didn't have a care in the world. I can't get her back. But just maybe, if she's lucky, Mallory will find her.

## SIGN ON THE DOTTED LINE

Children's parties are held at places where kids can run, climb, slide, scream, and basically work off all of the sugar from the cake and ice cream. These places tend to have names with the word "gym" in them, or words that imply serious perpetual motion like "pump" and "jump." What you end up with is a two-hour frenzy of kinetic motion that makes you wish you could unplug the little bastards.

What you end up with is a two-hour frenzy of kinetic motion that makes you wish you could unplug the little bastards.

Because most of these indoor play spaces involve an inherent amount of danger, parents must sign their children's lives away on a liability release. The print is very fine and hard to read, but basically it says something like: "I release the Pump and Jump Gym from all liability if my child falls and cracks his/her head open." The catch: If you don't sign, your kid doesn't play. And that's not an option.

So, like any good parent, I sign Mallory's life away, and then I spot her as if she were lifting 500-pound barbells. Everywhere she goes, I go. She's climbing the rope; I'm there. She's jumping into the pit of plastic balls; I'm there. She's coming down the zip line at about thirty-five miles per hour; I'm there. She's vaulting off the balance beam; I'm there. By the end of the party I'm exhausted and wondering why we gave up pin the tail on the donkey for this crap.

Kids are constantly getting hurt, falling into one another, hitting their heads on the equipment, tripping over things—and the parents just laugh it off and say, "He's just tired, poor little guy, missed his nap."

Hungover college students who probably know less about kids than they do about brain surgery are running the show. One college student connects your child to the zip line and sends her off at high speed to another college student at the other end. They sit on a stool and yell, "Hold on!" Each child appears shell-shocked, flying toward the wall with a deer-in-the-headlights look and a death grip on the wooden handle.

At one party there was an area called the cheese pit where children jump into a hole filled with pieces of foam. What you can't see from the side of the room is that the cheese pit is very deep. The foam doesn't actually come anywhere near the top of the pit. The initial drop is about ten feet. I found this out the hard way when I saw Chloe jump off the edge and then heard her muffled screams seconds later beneath layers of germy foam. Yes, as you probably can imagine, I was then forced to jump into the cheese pit myself. It was the first of about half-a-dozen cheese pit rescues during that particular party. We now decline invitations to the cheese pit place.

Recently, a place opened in our area that has large inflatable slides and mazes. The first time Chloe came down one of the slides, she shot off the end like a cannonball. At this moment I knew that I was on deck for the rest of the party. So, I spent the next two hours navigating inflatable corridors and shooting down inflatable slides with her on my lap.

It would be one thing if I was a mom in my twenties doing this, but I'm not. Let's just say I'm an older mother, albeit in very good shape, but I'm not sure anyone is in inflatable-slide-riding shape. I'm very sure that my mother never got in a moonwalk, on a trampoline, or on an amusement ride when I was growing up. Hell, when I was growing up, my mother couldn't swim or roller-skate, and wouldn't even set foot on an elevator, so I can guarantee she would never cruise down an inflatable slide.

At the end of the party, I felt like I had whiplash from contorting my body and hurling it at high speeds like a bobsled racer down a rubber chute. Then I realized that I never signed the form releasing the business from liability if *I* were to get injured. That's when my neck started *really* hurting.

## THE JOY OF GIVING

The hardest lesson for children to learn at a birthday party is that the gifts they are giving are not theirs to keep. Both of my girls love to help the hostess open her gifts at parties. They sit right at the foot of the birthday child and rip into the paper as if the gifts were theirs. I have to pull them back out of the circle of children and explain that it's not *their* birthday party.

Chloe inevitably wants to keep whatever gift she has given the birthday child. Not only is this embarrassing, but it also usually results in a scene in which the mother of the birthday child tells her to let Chloe play with the gift just to shut her up.

"Just let Chloe wear the fairy princess wings for a moment, Ashley," the mother says, trying to be polite through a clenched smile. Ashley naturally doesn't want to give up the fairy princess wings that she just received. Who would? This sends Chloe into a fit of rage on the floor. She is wearing the imperfect bejeweled crown she has just made and is holding a basketful of plastic eggs. The crown falls off and the plastic eggs go rolling down the driveway. This only increases her thrashing.

"Fine," I say, roughly pulling the straps over her little arms. "Put on the goddamn wings already!"

All the mothers are looking at me, actually *staring*. The gift opening and the party have come to a complete standstill. Everyone is paralyzed, frozen in time; my words hang in the air like a fart that everyone is trying to act like they don't smell. I am evil and now everyone knows my secret.

"I mean, Sweetie, let me help you put the wings on," I say. "You can wear them for a minute, but when you're done, you have to give them back, okay?" I pull her in for a bear hug. I realize this last bit about giving them back is going to promote more hysterics, so I lean in close to her and whisper in her little ear, "I'll get you your own frigging fairy wings on the way home if you just stop the whining."

Luckily, Mallory has gotten better about sharing the gifts as she gets older, so there is hope for Chloe. But now, my biggest worry with Mallory is that she will tell the birthday child we are re-gifting something. I am a champion re-gifter. I got the re-gifting gene from my mother, who has a gift drawer. I have a gift closet. For the most part I have an impeccable memory of who gave me what, and I try never to re-gift in the same circles. I know I've screwed up a few times. If you're one of the people who caught me, I'm sorry. But honestly, I only give away new stuff that's never been used that we don't need. It's just been wrapped, unwrapped, and rewrapped.

With kids' toys, re-gifting gets a little more complicated. We attend so many birthday parties, it's hard to keep everything straight. Now did Jill give us the Barbie or the clay? Was Phoebe there when Mallory opened it? Is it safe to re-gift? When in doubt, the answer is always *no*.

Sometimes I put away stuff not because we already have it but because I think kids in general get overwhelmed by too many new things at one time. I like to space the gifts out throughout the year. And occasionally when a birthday party creeps up and I haven't bought a gift, I take a dip in the gift closet. The key is that I must be stealthy because if Mallory catches me, there's hell to pay.

"Mommy, why did you give away my princess mirror and the magic set? I was going to play with them," she says as she teeters on the edge of a chair that she has somehow dragged into the gift closet so she can watch me organize, one of our favorite mother-daughter pastimes.

"Well, honey, we had those two birthday parties back-to-back and we needed gifts," I say as I pull her off the edge of the chair.

"Why don't you just buy the gifts like other mommies?" she says, wrapping her arms around my neck and her long legs around my waist. "Don't we have enough money to do that?"

"Ouch, wow, good point," I say. "Let me think about that one." I make a mental note to move the stuff from the gift closet somewhere she can't find it.

What's worse is when she calls me out in front of a group of people at a birthday party.

"Timmy, I hope you like the cool puzzle," she says. "I got it for my birthday, but I already had one just like it so Mommy said we should just give it to you." I pretend to be looking for something in my purse so that I can avoid eye contact with Timmy's mother.

Timmy doesn't give a flying you-know-what that Mallory is re-gifting the dinosaur puzzle. Timmy's mom, on the other hand, is probably making a mental note to cross Mallory off the next birthday party invitation list, which is fine with me. One less party means one less gift to wrap, one less exhausting afternoon, and one less goody bag to throw away.

## WHAT'S GOOD ABOUT GOODY BAGS?

Okay, I'm going to tell you right away this is going to sound un-American, but I hate goody bags. I hate giving them and receiving them. They are full of cheap junk—small plastic toys that break, toys that make noise, like kazoos or whistles, and candy that kids don't need after cake and ice cream. But for some reason this is junk they can't bear to part with, so it ends up crammed into drawers in their bedrooms. When the girls take an unexpected trip to Home Depot with their dad, I run through their rooms like a mad woman, stuffing all of this crap into a garbage bag. Inevitably this leads to a crisis.

When the girls take an unexpected trip to Home Depot with their dad, I run through their rooms like a mad woman, stuffing all of this crap into a garbage bag.

"Mommy, where is the purple glitter whistle I got at Andrea's party?" Mallory asks, hands on hips, lower lip in full-purse mode.

"Gee, honey, I'm not sure, we'll have to look for it," I say, trying not to meet her eyes.

"I just saw it in my drawer before I left for the store with Daddy," she says, taking her hands off her hips to rummage through the now-tidy drawer. "Why is my drawer so clean?"

She's onto me. She even knows that I stick the garbage bag in the hall closet to get it out of the way until I can safely stash it in the trash can outside.

"Mommy, why are my stuffed animals I won at the fair and my artwork from summer camp in a bag in the closet?" Mallory asks. "You're not throwing them away, are you?" She narrows her eyes at me, her hands up in the air, palms outstretched to God.

"No, honey, I was just organizing, I'm going to put everything back when I finish. I promise," I say.

But I'm on to her as well. She knows that all candy goes in the candy basket in the kitchen above the microwave so I can dole it out piece by piece as treats or desserts. Somewhere along the line Mallory decided if she could get the goody bag into her room and hide its contents, the candy would not end up in the communal basket. She decided she attends more parties than Chloe and therefore shouldn't have to share all the loot equally. So now I find candy wrappers under her bed, under her dresser, and smashed in with her stuffed animals.

The main reason I hate *giving* goody bags is that it's a pain in the ass to choose the items to go in them. Very few items are non-gender specific, which means you have to know exactly how many boys and how many girls are coming. Anyone who has ever had a child's birthday party knows that about half of the people you invite don't RSVP. I don't know how they were raised, but my mother responded to invitations immediately. Clearly, these women don't know my mother. For some reason many people find it difficult to follow through on this simple task. So you're left with no earthly idea who is coming.

The other thing I hate about the goody bag items is that they are overpriced, but yet you don't want to look cheap. You say, okay, one rubber bracelet, one beaded necklace, bubbles, and a lollipop. That's plenty, right? Not when Andrea's mom adds chocolate and stickers to this mix. Who does she think she is, putting six things in a goody bag and ruining it for the rest of us? But, of course, I give in. I pack the bag with junk that I don't want in my house, and yet I'm giving it to someone else's children so they can junk up their house.

My final issue with goody bags is stuffing them. You have to make sure every bag has the same number of items. This is critical; you can't make a mistake here.

"I got a glow stick, I got a glow stick," Joey chants, holding up the green prized possession.

"Wait a minute," Zach says, frantically rummaging through his bag. "I didn't get one, I didn't get a glow stick!" And he cries.

If parents waited until kids got into the car to let them open the goody bags, this would not be a problem, but clearly in our permissive age of parenting, this is not going to happen.

I'm also not good at transporting goody bags. They don't close unless you tie them with a ribbon—another very tedious venture. So you have to stand them up in a box and then try to not tip the box. Nothing, I mean nothing, is worse than a bunch of spilled goody bags. Seriously, that would push me over the edge.

I've thought about really rocking the boat one year and including things in the gift bag that *moms* would like to receive— like bath salts, Altoids, and a gift card for coffee. At least it's stuff someone could really use. Now that's a goody bag that deserves to be called good.

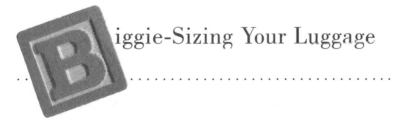

# iggie-Sizing Your Luggage

*"Adventure is worthwhile in itself."*
—Amelia Earhart

Before I had children I could pack a small duffel bag for a week. My mother says this is because my clothes are the size of a dinner napkin. But truthfully, it's because I'm a good packer. I choose a color, let's say black or brown, and coordinate every thing around that. I hate taking too much on a trip. I used to scoff at people in airports with oversized luggage because to me it signaled they were not seasoned travelers but simply imposters who were going on a cruise (the first one in their lives) paid for by a rich aunt.

With one child the duffel bag turned into a small *shared* suitcase. With two children the small suitcase morphed into a large suitcase. This goes against everything I believe in as a worldly traveler. At first I resisted. I would put everything in the suitcase that they needed— diapers, stuffed animals, dozens of cute outfits, and shoes to go with every cute outfit. But then there was absolutely no room for my stuff. I don't really need anything, I would kid myself. I'll just wear this one outfit every day and wash it. I contemplated wearing running shoes out to dinner. But then I face the grim reality that I might actually have to use a bigger bag.

I unpack and repack until I can achieve some balance of cute girl outfits and what I really, really need, like underwear and socks. I start this complex process at least a week in advance of the trip. Usually the living room serves as what Grif refers to as the staging area. In the staging area there are several piles. There are the things we need to take, the things we want to take, and the things that probably won't fit. Every day I look at the stuff that won't fit and I delete something. Good packing, like a good life, is all about knowing what to leave out.

> Good packing, like a good life, is all about knowing what to leave out.

This packing nightmare is mine and mine alone. Early on in our marriage Grif and I divided tasks. I am officially "the family organizer," keeping straight everything from suitcases to kitchen drawers. When I ask Grif why this has become solely my responsibility, he says, "Because you're so good at it."

Luckily, I do not have to pack *his* suitcase, which he does ten to fifteen minutes before we walk out the door. He packs too much, his oversized luggage bulging. Still, it never fails. He always forgets something.

"Honey, have you seen my bathing suit?" Grif asks me in the hotel room.

"No, did you pack it?"

"I guess not."

"I can't imagine why you would have thought to bring a bathing suit to the beach."

How did he survive thirty-three years without me?

. . . . . . . . . . . . . . . . . . . . . . . . . . . . . . . . . . . . . . .

## TRAVEL GEEKS

Before I had kids, I used to see those people with big luggage boxes on the top of their cars and think they were *crazy*.

"How much stuff could they possibly have?" I asked Grif. "I mean, what do they have in those things, dead bodies?"

I heard the guy at our Volvo dealership refer to those boxes as mother-in-law containers one time, because they are large enough to fit a human being.

"Wait until we have kids," he said. "I bet we'll need it."

"Well, I will never have one of those things," I said. "And I'll never have a minivan."

"We'll see," he said. "We'll see."

Guess what, I have one, a big honking plastic box on top of my car. I am officially a travel geek. The breaking point came when we packed for our first long trip to Philadelphia to see my parents. I was trying to fit luggage, a portable crib, a stroller, diapers, a cooler, a collapsible high chair, a potty seat, Christmas presents, and God knows what else into the back of a Volvo station wagon. I realized at this point it was either a minivan or a luggage box. I opted for the luggage box.

Not unlike the actual packing process, the car packing process has also landed squarely in my lap. If it were up to Grif to pack the car, it would be done minutes before we pulled out of the driveway. That's an additional stressor that I can't add to my already overflowing plate of red-hot anxiety. Besides, if he can't make something fit, his reaction is to leave it behind.

"Do we really need the pack-and-play?" he asked. "I mean, can't she just sleep with us?"

"No, she can't sleep with us, that *has* to go in," I say, standing my ground.

"Okay, what about the stroller, can't she just walk when we go places?"

I give up and send him inside to make coffee. *That* he can do. I can make it all fit. I have the power. It's one of the many magic tricks that mothers have in their repertoires, the ability to make lots of stuff fit into small spaces.

It's like a puzzle where every piece has a fixed spot, but if you put something in the wrong place, nothing else fits. One of the major issues is making sure anything you might need during the trip—like food, drinks, and the DVD player—is accessible, So of course I have three piles— things that I don't need during the trip (things that go up top), things that I may need (like extra clothes), and things we do need (like snacks, water, and DVDs).

> I can make it all fit. I have the power.

I guess most husbands pack cars.

"Wow, your husband sure is lucky," a guy said to me in the parking lot of our rented beach house as he watched me hurl bags into the luggage box. "Do you change the oil, too?"

"No," I said sweetly. "And I don't cook or iron either."

## TRULY STUPID AIRHEADS (T.S.A.)

I started flying with Mallory when she was an infant. Until they're two, kids fly free as long as they sit on a parent's lap. It seemed shameful not to take advantage of this perk. I brought bottles, pacifiers, snacks, toys, books. Like a Sherpa, I lugged all my gear onto the plane with Mallory attached to my chest in the baby carrier. I was prepared for anything.

But then I discovered that when you're traveling alone and you have a baby on your hip, folding a stroller with one hand and your feet can be tricky. One time in my anxiety-laden struggle to do it myself, I tripped on the edge of my coat and fell in the walkway area just as I tried to step off the plane. Everyone just looked at me and stared. No one offered a hand. It was like a scene out of a movie where someone gets killed in the street while everyone watches, and later when the police interview people about why they didn't help, everyone says it's because they thought someone else would do it.

My hatred of flying with children really escalated after 9/11. That's when traffic jams on Interstate 95 and flipping Goldfish to screaming children in the backseat started to seem like a better alternative. At least in a car I was in control. At the airport we all know who is in control—the T.S.A., definitely not us.

Not unlike federal postal workers who are trained to go by the book and not ever think out of the box, the airport screeners are single-minded in the way they deal with the public. It's like they're on autopilot and there's no deviation, I mean *no* deviation, from their playbook.

The stress of taking off my children's coats, shoes, belts, removing my laptop, and making sure no one runs away or gets snatched by a stranger is enough to make me think about taking a bus.

One time when Mallory was three, the screener asked her to walk through the metal detector without me. I repeatedly told her to wait for me on the other side. The screener then funneled me into another line in the opposite direction of where Mallory was standing. Bravely, risking a body-cavity search, I refused to go in any direction that would put any more distance between me and my child. The screener was clearly reading from a page in the T.S.A. rule book, which clearly guarantees no special rights for parents traveling alone with children. She seemed flabbergasted when I refused her direct order to get in the other line. I wanted to hit her over the head with her little handheld metal-detecting wand, but I held back.

On another occasion, when Chloe was just two months old, I flew with her to Pennsylvania because my mother was having some minor outpatient knee surgery and needed my help. As I stepped up to the security line, the screener told me to take off my baby carrier and run it through the machine. When I got to the other side, there was no way for me to put the carrier back on and hold the baby at the same time. I couldn't put a two-month-old baby down on the floor, so I asked the screener if he could help.

"We're only allowed to assist people who are disabled," he said to me, reciting a line that sounded like it was verbatim from the T.S.A. handbook.

"A parent traveling alone with an infant *is* disabled," I said to his impassive face. Luckily, an older woman stepped up and held Chloe while I reattached the baby carrier to my chest. She rolled her eyes and scoffed at the T.S.A. official who refused to help.

On my return trip from Philadelphia to Raleigh, I called for special assistance. When the woman from the airlines arrived with a wheelchair, I told her I simply needed her help holding my baby when I went through security. Being a person who had the ability to think outside the box, in addition to a person with ovaries, she ditched the wheelchair and gladly obliged.

I know that by bashing airport screeners I'm risking even more body-cavity searches, but I figure the chances that any of them are reading this book are pretty small. Especially when it takes so much time to memorize their own rules.

. . . . . . . . . . . . . . . . . . . . . . . . . . . . . . . . . . . . . . . . .

## NOTHING TO FEAR BUT A POOP BOMB

Recently, I flew alone with Chloe to Philadelphia. The second they closed the doors and pulled onto the runway, she screamed, *"I've gotta poop!"*

I tried to calmly explain to her that we were about to take off and that we couldn't get out of our seats, but she just kept screaming, *"The poop is coming, it's coming out."*

Finally, I rang the flight attendant's bell and asked her if we could get up for a moment.

"If you do, it's at your own risk," she said with a robotlike tone in her voice. She had obviously used this line many times before. But what about the risk to everyone else of having a poop bomb stink up the plane?

I decided it was worth the risk, and we hurried to the airplane bathroom. Chloe sat on the potty for about the length of time it would take me to read two sections of the Sunday edition of the *New York Times*. When we flush the toilet—you know the flush, the one that sounds like it's going to suck your intestines out through your butt—she jumped into my arms in fear, knocking my head sharply against the bathroom door.

"Everything okay in there?" the flight attendant asked in a monotone voice. I am convinced that she's in the wrong line of work, that the T.S.A. will probably be knocking at her door any day now, trying to recruit her.

"Just fine," I said as I struggled to my feet with Chloe firmly attached to my neck. She hung on for dear life with her pants around her ankles.

As soon as we returned to our seats and fastened our seat belts, Chloe started screaming again: *"I want orange juice. I need orange juice."* I whispered that Mommy didn't have any orange juice and that we would have to wait until the plane took off before the flight attendants started serving drinks. We were still sitting on the tarmac delayed for God knows what reason. The flight attendant who was strapped into her seat a few feet from us stared into space, ignoring Chloe's pleas. *"I'm thirsty. My mouth is yucky. I need orange juice,"* she continued.

Finally, the pilot came over the loudspeaker.

"Folks, it looks like we're next in line for takeoff. Thanks for your patience. Please make sure your tray tables are up and your seats are in an upright position," he said in a Top Gun voice.

In my head I added one line: "And please, someone get that frigging kid in seat 3B a goddamn orange juice before I lose it!"

. . . . . . . . . . . . . . . . . . . . . . . . . . . . . . . . . . . . . . . .

## MADDIE-NESS

Since my children were born, we have been taking them to the Jersey Shore, where my father and his wife have a house. We spend one week with them in a rented house nearby because they don't do kids underfoot. We spend another week with my mother, Maddie, in a rented house in a nearby beach town. This, of course, is the visitation agreement worked out by my parents for their forty-year-old daughter.

I think I've already alluded to my mother's obsessive-compulsive behavior. Ultimately it's her problem, but when we take a vacation with her, it becomes everybody's problem.

She adores my children, who call her Maddie. She stocks our rental home in Cape May with their favorite foods. She comes bearing gifts—toys, books, and new outfits for the girls. She rents this awesome house that was definitely decorated by gay men who love Pottery Barn as much as I do. She goes way beyond her calling both as a mother and a grandmother.

But living with two small children for a week is enough to drive Maddie *mad*.

From sandy feet in the den, to the melted popsicles on the porch, to wet bathing suits on the bed, it's all she can do to breathe deeply and stay calm. She cleans constantly, putting me in a perpetual cycle of anxiety mixed with a chaser of guilt.

When we go out to dinner, the girls inevitably have tantrums and embarrass her. Maddie and I order another bottle of wine and pour the leftovers in to-go cups for the walk home.

This, of course, is the visitation agreement worked out by my parents for their forty-year-old daughter.

One evening I was delicately cutting my tomatoes and mozzarella, while, from the back of the restaurant, Chloe was screaming in the bathroom, where she was curled up in a ball on the floor for no particular reason. Despite my coaxing she refused to leave. So *I* left.

"Mom, could you get Chloe, please?" I ask, still cutting.

I dab the corners of my mouth with my napkin as other diners look at me in horror that I am ignoring my child's cries from the restroom. *Walk a mile in my shoes, people,* I think.

"What happened?" my mom says, getting up in no real hurry.

"She got too much soap on her hands," I say in between bites. "She's mad."

"Okay, back in a flash," my mom says, already sauntering toward the bathroom to rescue Chloe from the soap. Other diners point toward the bathroom as if she couldn't just follow the banshee screams.

Sometimes grandmothers have to pick up the slack when mothers simply can't handle the moment.

Maddie comes out holding Chloe in her arms, talking to her in a quiet, soothing voice. Chloe's face is red and tear-stained, but there is a little smile forming at the corners of her mouth. I often wonder if the grandmother gene is something you inherit from your mother. I sure hope so.

ommy Wants to Quit Ballet

*"If you do not tell the truth about yourself you cannot
tell it about other people."*
—Virginia Woolfe

PLEASE MAKE SURE SIBLINGS SIT QUIETLY IN THE LOBBY DURING
CLASS read the sign on the glass doors of the ballet studio. DO
NOT MOVE THE CHAIRS. NO EATING OR DRINKING IN THE LOBBY.
This, along with the fact that my five-year-old was required to
wear a very specific outfit, have her hair in a bun, and stay ab-
solutely quiet during class all pointed to one thing—clearly,
Mommy wasn't going to survive ballet.

When we first signed up for ballet, I had Angelina Ballerina
in mind. Angelina is a mouse who performs ballet with her
mouse friends. They wear tutus, carry wands, and can be awkward at times, as mice tend to be when performing complicated
ballet steps, but they always have a good time. Somewhere
along the line the folks at our dance studio skipped over Angelina and went right to Swan Lake.

I was never exposed to ballet as a child. It would have required my mother to spend time and energy on an activity she
thought at odds with feminism. But secretly, I always thought

ballet might be kind of fun. So when Mallory begged me to enroll her in a class, I bought the $78 outfit and put together a sloppy bun out of her pageboy haircut with a thousand bobby pins and a full can of hairspray.

When we first started ballet, things were a lot looser. We mothers sat on the floor, socialized with each other, read the newspaper, talked on cell phones. When babies came along, they crawled around the lobby, ate Cheerios and yogurt, and banged on the glass to wave at their big sisters. But somewhere along the line the ballet school cracked down on us. I guess they thought that we were mocking the entire process through our actions. Clearly, we weren't supposed to be having fun. This was serious business: Molding little prima ballerinas wasn't going to be easy; no one said it would be. What were we thinking? That's when the rules went up.

Unlike other mothers who sat quietly knitting in the lobby or planning playdates, I now dropped Mallory off. I couldn't handle the looks I would get if I tried to brave the entire forty-five-minute class with an unruly sibling in the lobby. The few times I tried it, Chloe ran wild while her peers sat quietly coloring or paging through books. She tapped on the glass and waved frantically at Mallory through the cracked Venetian blinds designed to keep distractions to a minimum. She crushed stray raisins and Cheerios from her pockets into the carpet. She insisted on using the water fountain on high power until it soaked both of us.

She'd run away from me, up and down in front of the classroom door, stopping only to press her lips against the glass and occasionally bang on it, yelling at the top of her lungs: "SISSY!"

All of a sudden I came to a dramatic realization: I wasn't having fun anymore. I wanted to quit ballet. Luckily, after three years of ballet, Mallory decided that she was ready to move on to other activities and hang up her ballet shoes for good. First, however, she wanted to finish out the year. And it isn't all about me, is it? It's about her. So I agreed to let her finish. After all, we had pre-paid.

"Mommy, we can't be quitters," she said with her hands on her hips. "Remember you always finish what you start. Right?"

How could I argue with that? Well, I could, I can argue with anything, but it wouldn't be right.

. . . . . . . . . . . . . . . . . . . . . . . . . . . . . . . . . . . . . . . . .

## THE ANTI-EVERYTHING MOM

One of the biggest fallacies about putting kids in activities when they are young is that you are doing it *for them*. I learned early on that many parents actually put their kids in activities for their own benefit. They want a social outlet, a way to meet other parents of young children and talk about how crazy their lives are. This is especially true for stay-at-home moms who are desperate to talk about anything besides Barney. I can totally understand this.

My plate is so full it's spilling over the edges onto the floor and pooling around my aching feet. Between work, my family, the house, and an active social life, I have trouble figuring out when to fit in time to pee. I can barely keep up with the people I really like, so the thought of spending time with people I just kind of like is about as appealing as getting laser eye surgery without valium. What I am looking for is a little peace and quiet. If I do take my child to an activity without her younger sister, I simply want to be left alone to read the paper, do the crossword puzzle, or respond to unimportant e-mails on my Blackberry. To other mothers, this makes me The Anti-Mom.

The Anti-Mom is snubbed in subtle ways. I am reluctantly asked to simply bring cream cheese to the end-of-season soccer party because the real soccer moms assume I probably can't handle anything else. I'm sure someone has been assigned to bring backup cream cheese lest I forget and then God forbid the kids might have to eat their bagels dry. The truth is that I can handle cream cheese and then some. I have a friend who once said, "If you need someone to do something, ask a busy person." That's me. Ask me to do something and it gets done. But the soccer moms wouldn't know this about me because they don't ask.

*If you need someone to do something, ask a busy person.*

When the mothers at an activity plan playdates at the park or at a local coffee shop after the class, they shun The Anti-Mom by talking in hushed tones.

I whisper, "A three-letter word for a female sheep . . ."

I overhear, "Hey, do you guys want to meet at Ritter Park afterwards?" The organizer glances furtively in my direction.

"Ewe, that's it, ewe," I say aloud to prove that my crossword puzzle is much more interesting than their little gathering. The truth is I'm six years old again in gym class not getting picked for a hot game of dodgeball.

"Great, the kids will love it," she says, and then glances toward me again.

"Flightless bird," I say under my breath. "Emu, obviously."

They reserve their best sideways glances for when I answer my cell phone with my business voice and then, imagine

my gall, actually conduct business while my daughter is dancing, or kicking a ball, or whatever she is doing. I guess they
think that if I'm on the phone for a few minutes, I don't care
about my child.

I admit, sometimes I can understand how they might find
my work conversations less than palatable. "How many gunshot
wounds are there? I see. Well, how long do they think the body
has been there?"

Then it's my turn to give a few sideways glances to see if
they're listening. Of course they are, but they turn away quickly
so they don't look like they are. It's childish, I know, to play the
my-life-is-more-exciting-than-your-life game. But sometimes
it's all I've got.

## ALL IN THE FAMILY

It took me awhile to realize that children's activities are not only
about *mothers* who need friends. Apparently, *entire families* are
looking for new people to hang out with and drink beer with on
the weekends. I had no idea that soccer was a form of
match.com for families looking for Barney and Betty Rubble to
join their backyard barbecues.

Mallory's first experience with soccer was born out of a mis-
calculation on my part. Even though my husband and I have no
team-sport DNA, somehow I thought she might have received
an errant gene from another part of the pool. In fact, I played (if
you can call it that) soccer so poorly as a child, it makes my
heart race with anxiety just thinking about it. It's like a wicked
drug flashback.

I'm constantly amazed at how God allows history to repeat
itself in traits that don't seem to be inheritable. Along with my

I-hate-soccer gene, Mallory also got a new strain that must have come from her father, the I-refuse-to-even-pretend-to-like-it gene.

I spent most of the time on the sidelines trying to keep baby Chloe from crawling onto the field. Like the serious ballet mothers, I got a lot of ugly looks from the serious soccer families. Although the soccer practice lasted just an hour, these people looked like they were prepared to camp in the wilderness for a month. They had umbrellas, coolers, cold drinks, and towels to wipe the brows of their star players. They had cameras, binoculars, sunscreen, hats, and snacks. I had my cell phone on my hip and a bottle of water for the three of us to share.

**Being a Yankee in the South automatically makes you a bitch until it's proven that you are actually a nice person.**

It probably made the situation worse that I showed up in a baseball hat, flip-flops, and cutoffs with no makeup. But because I'm in local television, they knew who I was, and so automatically my unwillingness to conform to their soccer culture made me a snob. It's kind of like how being a Yankee in the South automatically makes you a bitch until it's proven that you are actually a nice person. I'm still waiting for the latter.

The time I did break form and brought a chair, it was useless. I spent the hour chasing Chloe as she crawled onto the field, soccer balls barely missing her head. There was no time to sit. Mallory, however, found another use for the chair. In between her moments on the field, she would hide behind it, hoping the coach would not see her when it was time to go back into the game. She is definitely her mother's daughter. She told me that it was too hot, she needed shade, and was tired of all that running. When I asked her why she didn't try to kick the ball, she said, "Why should I, Mommy? Everyone else is kicking it."

Not only was she right about not expending energy kicking a ball when everyone else was trying to do the same thing, but she was also bringing me back to that eight-year-old girl who felt the same way. Who knew DNA could be so specific in its replication?

Mallory spent most of her time on the field talking to opposing players about cool purple hair clips, or squatting and looking at the blue painted grass along the sidelines. It didn't bother me so much that she didn't want to play. It bothered me that she didn't want to play and now we were stuck doing this every Saturday until May.

But, like the ballet thing, I sucked it up and decided to finish it out. Subliminally, I think I wanted to expose my kid to a game I sucked at so that I could possibly redeem my own poor athletic career. But, unliked me, Mallory *could* be a good soccer player if she wanted to, it just isn't her thing.

When it came time for the end-of-season awards ceremony, the soccer parents sent a representative to talk to me about helping with the after-party. I imagined they drew straws to decide which one would approach me.

Out of the corner of my eye I see her coming. Self-consciously, I tucked my stray greasy hairs beneath my baseball cap and tugged several strings off the edges of my jean shorts. I looked down at my chipped pink toenails and made a mental note to get a pedicure.

"Hi, I'm Bitsy," she says. "And you are?"

She tilts her head and makes a knowing side glance to her friends in Bermuda shorts, not cute shorts, by the way. Too-high-in-the-waist shorts. *Mom* shorts.

"Amanda," I said, extending my hand with a forced smile. Chloe dangles from my hip. "It's nice to meet you."

"We were wondering," Bitsy said, motioning to the other moms, "if you would like to participate in the end-of-season awards banquet and party?"

She drops her mouth open as if expecting to hear me say no.

"Sure, whatever," I say like I'm in junior high. "I mean sure. That would be great!" I say, mustering my best fake I'm-glad-to-help-out response.

"Cream cheese, that's your assignment," Bitsy says with her hands on her hips. "Not regular cream cheese, Cleo is already bringing that. Something different like pineapple or strawberry."

Who eats that fancy cream cheese? Certainly not four-year-olds.

"Sure, no problem," I say. "I'll bring the cream cheese, you can count on me. Anything else?"

She looked down but then quickly looked away as she noted the chipped polish on my toenails. She wrung her perfectly manicured hands.

"Well, there is one other thing," Bitsy said. "A check, we're all pitching in to buy the kids trophies and the coach a gift certificate. It's going to be $18.50, if you want to participate, that is—you don't have to."

Sure, I'll be the only jerk who doesn't pitch in for the trophies and the gift certificate. When they call my daughter's name, they'll say: "Mallory—oh, wait a second, sorry, Mallory, no trophy for you. Your mom didn't pitch in." Then I think maybe she thinks I can't afford the $18.50. After all, I am wearing cutoffs and flip-flops with a chipped pedicure.

"No problem," I say again. "Who do I write the check to?"

Bitsy steps backward, obviously surprised she achieved her goal. She rushes back to the other moms with the check, and someone gives her a high five. Mission accomplished.

. . . . . . . . . . . . . . . . . . . . . . . . . . . . . . . . . . . . . . . . . . .

## PLAY IT AGAIN, MALLORY

Piano was my husband's idea. He plays piano, trumpet, and drums. His current band is called the Funk Daddies. It's a bunch of fathers who work during the week and on the weekends take their midlife crisis out in someone's garage. Personally, I think it's a better alternative than an Internet hooker or an expensive sports car. I played piano for about thirty seconds when I was seven, but—not unlike my fifteen-second smoking habit when I was fourteen—it didn't take.

The drums are Grif's real passion, but just like dancers believe ballet is the root of all dance, Grif believes piano is the root of all music.

> Just like dancers believe ballet is the root of all dance, Grif believes piano is the root of all music.

We chose our first piano teacher for Mallory because she was in our neighborhood. She had been teaching kids for twenty years, and she was Greek. For some reason that made me feel good. Her name was Dora, which is a big plus for a kid who has been raised watching Dora the Explorer. Mallory, who likes very few people on first meeting, immediately took to Dora.

Dora insisted that a parent accompany Mallory to her lesson so that we understood her methods and could help her practice. What a joke. The only thing I know about music is how to download it. I carry a tune like Linda McCartney in "Hey Jude," God rest her soul. I can't read a note of music. The only thing I know about piano is that Elton John plays it really well. So in short, Dora might just as well have been speaking Greek to me in trying to teach me how to teach my daughter to play piano. I don't understand either one.

I spent the first few lessons trying to keep baby Chloe from crawling underneath Dora's coffee table. Meanwhile, Dora was instructing me in how to practice the songs with Mallory, completely forgetting that I know nothing about music even though I kept telling her. But, just like anyone else completely immersed in a passion, she couldn't imagine a person with so little musical ability. It was something she couldn't comprehend no matter how many different ways I expressed this to her.

"Dora, I'm really not sure I'm following you, maybe you should write these instructions down for my husband. He reads music," I would remind her. "I don't."

"No, no," she would say, waving me off with her thick Greek accent that had not faded even after decades in this country. "It's *easy*. Just do this sequence three times, hold the note here, and don't forget to start at the top."

I finally made a deal with Grif, that music is his thing, and so piano lessons with his daughter should also be his thing. I mean, I have plenty of things on my plate. I handle the ballet thing, the playdate thing, the birthday party thing, the reading before bed thing, the volunteering at school thing, and the list goes on.

By default, practicing with Mallory at night is also his thing. Unfortunately, he has a mini-Mozart complex with his daughter. I hear her screaming from the other room: "I can't do it, it's too hard!" Then I find her curled up beneath the piano bench, refusing to play. Call me crazy, but I'm pretty perceptive; this does not look productive to me. Once again I picture her in the therapist's office someday.

"He made me do it," Mallory would say. "He pushed me to play until I cried. I can't even listen to the radio today. I hate music. Child abuse is what it was. And my mother did nothing to stop it!"

If Grif is out, I practice with her. I tell her everything sounds good because I don't know any better. It's like watching someone drive a stick shift car, something I can't do, I'm like wow, you know how to play piano with two hands at the same time? She smiles and beams with pride. She knows that I am a blissfully ignorant music critic.

> She knows that I am a blissfully ignorant music critic.

"That wasn't perfect, Mommy; let me play that one again." I just nod and tell her everything sounds great. Okay, so maybe I'm not grooming a little Mozart, but I think I'm getting a lot of points in the good karma department. I look for the love any way I can get it.

At one point Grif got fed up with the daily fights with Mallory about practicing piano. He told her that if she didn't want to play anymore, she could quit. But the truth is she's a very good piano player. Her new teacher, Miss Marie (who is from South Africa; for some reason we hire only imported piano teachers), thinks she has "it." I've never had "it" in anything I do. I'm not trying to be a martyr; honestly, I may have a lot of little bits and pieces of "it," but not like Mallory does when it comes to musical ability.

Also there's a little part of me that wishes I had not quit piano. There's the what-if factor. Could I have been good? I visualize myself at a party and someone asks me if I can play a few songs. I have the same fantasy about playing guitar for a group of people on the spur of the moment, everyone sitting cross-legged in a circle at my feet. "Gather round," I say to the group. "Any requests? I can play just about anything."

My missed opportunities to wow crowds with my musical ability made me question Mallory's decision to quit.

**Finally, I dug deep and pulled out the only thing I had left.**

I gave her all the standard talking points: Don't quit what you've started, everything worth doing in life is hard work, and you may actually like it in the end. My speech was so lame, even I didn't believe it. Finally, I dug deep and pulled out the only thing I had left.

"Come on, Sweetie, it's really important to your dad," I said, tucking strands of her brown hair behind her ear. "He'll be so bummed out if you quit."

"Okay, I'll try it again," she said through clenched teeth. And she's still trying.

# pilogue

Mallory just joined the Y-Princesses (in my day it was called Indian Princesses, which must no longer be politically correct). Y-Princesses are like Girl Scouts, except fathers are the troop leaders, and the girls get to wear much cooler clothes. I did it with my dad when I was growing up in Pennsylvania. The only thing I can really remember about it is one lame camping trip where we painted our faces and didn't catch any fish. The only thing my dad can remember is the same lame camping trip where he got really drunk with the other dads (unbeknownst to me) and didn't catch any fish. Today, unlike in my day, Princesses are serious business for both dads and daughters.

> Neurosis flows down my family tree like sap.

When Grif came home from the first organizational meeting, he told Mallory she needed to pick a name in order to be part of the tribe. This sent her into a tailspin of anxiety. Neurosis flows down my family tree like sap.

After thinking about it for a while, she ran into our room

bursting with excitement. "I've got it Mommy—*Angela!* Angela will be my name."

I had to steady myself on the dresser to keep from bursting into laughter. There's nothing that upsets Mallory more than thinking someone is laughing at her, and I can relate. So I tried really hard not to show how tickled I was.

"Sweetie, it has to be an Indian name," I said.

"Oh," she said with apparent recognition. "Like Nashada from my class last year?"

I had to turn away to keep her from seeing my quivering cheeks.

"No, honey, not India the country," I said. "Indian as in Native American."

I pulled her in tight for a hug and she buried her face just beneath my chest. It's only a matter of time before her head will rest on my shoulder. She will probably be taller than me someday, a someday that is right around the corner. Even at the end of a day, when my stockings have a run, and I'm still in my suit and heels, wiping boogers and reading stories, I know: It won't last forever, no matter how hard I wish it would.

That's why it so important for me not only to remember but also to record these precious moments. They are gems, nuggets chipped away from the parenting journey and delicately stored. Or maybe like scraps of fabric that pieced together make one big, crazy patchwork quilt. It is an imperfect quilt that is worn and faded in some spots. It might smother you at times, but ultimately it keeps you warmer at night than a roaring fire.

When my kids grow up and ask me what they were like as children, they'll read this book and get a sense of their history, the good and the bad. I'm sure they will be embarrassed by some of what I've shared. But eventually, they will understand it was all written by a hopelessly flawed mother who somehow created two hopelessly perfect children.

Mallory, Flying Horse, and her father, Blowing Horn, will spend many precious moments with The Daughters of the Sun tribe over the next few years. But in my heart, she will always be Angela.

# ABOUT THE AUTHOR

courtesy Jennifer Robertson

Amanda Lamb is an award-winning television reporter covering the crime beat for WRAL-TV, a CBS affiliate in Raleigh, North Carolina. She had every intention of making it *really* big. But something funny happened on her way up the career ladder—her life. Amanda married a metals recycler with roots firmly planted in the Tarheel State. Soon they had a mortgage, a car payment, and within the span of just a few years, two little girls.

Amanda's career as a journalist has allowed her many opportunities—interviewing presidents, flying in fighter jets, scuba-diving with sharks, covering hurricanes. More of what she has to say about parenting is regularly featured on the Web site dot-moms.com, a worldwide community of women writers. Amanda's writing also appears in *This Day in the Life*. Her candid, touching chapter opens the powerful, critically acclaimed collection of day diaries from thirty-four women across the country.